Tim Duncan: The Inspiring Story of Basketball's Greatest Power Forward

An Unauthorized Biography

By: Clayton Geoffreys

Visit my website at www.claytongeoffreys.com
Cover photo by Zereshk is licensed under CC BY 2.0 / modified from original

Table of Contents

Foreword

Tim Duncan solidified his NBA legacy years ago; easily a future Hall of Famer, Tim Duncan provides us with many lessons on the power of hard work, persistence, and leadership. In a league filled with diva superstars demanding maximum contracts, Tim Duncan has always put the San Antonio Spurs ahead of himself, so much so that Duncan cut his salary in half in 2012-2013 just to keep the San Antonio Spurs team together. The epitome of a class act, Tim Duncan has never been a showy NBA superstar, but what he has done for the Spurs over his career has made him easily the greatest power forward to ever play the game. Thank you for purchasing *Tim Duncan: The Inspiring Story of Basketball's Greatest Power Forward*. In this unauthorized biography, we will learn Tim's incredible life story and impact on the game of basketball. Hope you enjoy and if you do, please do not forget to leave a review! Also, check out my website at claytongeoffreys.com to join my exclusive list where I let you know about my latest books and give you goodies!

Cheers,

Clayton Geoffreys

Visit me at www.claytongeoffreys.com

Introduction

When Napoleon Bonaparte returned from Elba to France in the Hundred Days, an aide told him how gratifying it must have been to see the Paris crowds cheer his return. Napoleon shook his head. Those same crowds, he noted, had less than three days ago been cheering for the now departed King of France.

This historical story is a perfect description of Tim Duncan and the San Antonio Spurs, who at this point, have dominated the NBA for longer than Napoleon ruled the French. Today, the Spurs are beloved by everyone. They play the right way: the fundamental way. The Spurs offense is flawlessly executed as they feed open shots to their players and transform players who barely seemed to belong in the NBA into valuable team members. Even though no single Spur has averaged more than 30 minutes per game in the 2013-14 season, no one complains about minutes or a lack of shots. They buy into the Spurs' system which ensures that everyone gets plenty of down-time over the course of the long NBA season.

Tim Duncan would sit in the front row to praise San Antonio's system. He is acclaimed by many as the greatest player of his generation, and NBA players, media personalities, and fans alike are virtually unanimous in praising him. In Game 7 of the 2013 NBA Finals, Duncan missed a crucial layup in the final minute, slapped the floor in frustration, and was on the verge of tears in the postgame press conference while answering for the loss and for San Antonio's ultimate defeat. For other stars, such a sequence would be viewed as fragility and a lack of clutchness. For Duncan however, in light of everything he has accomplished and who he is, no one complained; in fact, the floor slap has been used as a sign of Duncan's greatness. That single outburst of emotion spoke volumes coming from such a stoic man. Had it been anyone else that had done it, such a display of raw emotion would have likely been overlooked or criticized. Through great personality and expert game play, Tim Duncan has elevated the Spurs to stand amongst the top of the Western Conference for over a decade.

This is incredible for those of us who recognize that a half-decade ago, the Spurs were the most hated team in the league. In the eyes of the media and fans alike, they were not the brilliant and beautifully effective team that executed basketball to a level which no other team could. They were an unpopular, defense-first, and an essentially boring team that never hesitated to use dirty tricks, flop, or work the referees to be a more exciting, fun team , similar to the "Seven Seconds or Less" Phoenix Suns. Bruce Bowen was considered a nasty piece of work who would kick an opposing player in the face if he could get away with it, while Robert Horry hip-checked Steve Nash into the stands during the playoffs, and Manu Ginobili was generally deemed a cowardly flopper. Duncan may not have received quite the same ire as his teammates, but he was boring. A superstar without a doubt, but one who got to play on stacked teams, unlike Kevin Garnett and Kobe Bryant, who struggled on mediocre teams in the mid-2000s.

One may wonder if the Spurs care about the fact that those who love them today are also those who castigated them in the past. The answer is clear: not in the slightest. They just keep winning one 50-game season after another, chasing championships and glory. Right in the middle of that, Tim Duncan, oblivious to the roars or boos of the crowd, continues to play with the same efficiency and genius that he has brought to the NBA over the past 18 years of his career.

Chapter 1: Childhood and Early Life

Timothy Theodore Duncan was born on April 25, 1976, to William and Ione Duncan. Duncan was raised in St. Croix, a small island that is part of the U.S. Virgin Islands, located just east of Puerto Rico. The Duncan's were a tall, athletic family. Had Tim and his two elder sisters, Cheryl and Tricia, grown up in the continental United States, they might have played basketball, baseball, or some other team sports. Out in the Caribbean, they swam. Cheryl, the older sister, was a strong swimmer in her own right, but it was Tricia and Tim who would truly gain renown in the water. Tricia competed for the Virgin Islands in the 1988 Olympics, and at age 13, Tim Duncan was one of the best swimmers in the entire United States. Even at a young age, he already possessed the focus and mental poise which he would be famous for throughout his storied NBA career. His best event as a young swimmer was the 400 meter freestyle, arguably the most challenging swimming race from a mental standpoint. He was also a highly intelligent child who skipped the third grade. Whenever Duncan swam, his mother Ione was there, cheering him on and timing him to help him improve even more. At the age of 13, one of the greatest NBA players of all time had never touched a basketball, and spent his days dreaming of swimming for the United States in the 1992 Barcelona Olympics. Tricia, Tim's Olympic swimmer older sister, was convinced that Duncan would eventually surpass her.

In the fall of 1989, everything changed when Duncan's mother was diagnosed with breast cancer. She continued her work as a midwife for the next few months, but on April 24, 1990, one day before Tim Duncan turned fourteen, she passed away. In her last moments, she made Tim promise that he would go to college and earn a degree. On top of that, Hurricane Hugo, the most damaging hurricane at that point in US history, struck St. Croix on September 17, 1989.

Duncan slept through most of the storm, but in addition to ravaging the entire island, Hugo destroyed the only Olympic-sized swimming pool in St. Croix. The only way for Duncan to train was to swim in the open ocean, but the normally calm boy was terrified of the possibility of sharks. With his mother gone, and with no place to swim, Tim Duncan lost his motivation. He never swam competitively again. Instead, he turned to something which had survived the hurricane – a basketball goal which was a Christmas present from his oldest sister Cheryl.

Cheryl had been living in Columbus, Ohio, but she moved back to St. Croix with her husband Ricky Lowery shortly after her mother's death. Lowery had played basketball for a Division III school, and began to coach Tim Duncan in basketball. Duncan had just joined St. Dunstan's Episcopal High School, and was already around six feet tall. Lowery guessed that Duncan would be 6'4'' or 6'5'' by the time he finished growing, and focused his teaching on perimeter guard skills. However, Duncan grew nine more inches during his high school years. After easily making the high-school basketball team as a freshman, he developed into a player with both the skills of a guard and a big man, showcasing himself to be the best player in the Virgin Islands, if not the entire Caribbean.

Back then, no one was paying any attention to basketball players outside of the continental United States, where the best players competed against each other in national tournaments and in the Amateur Athletic Union (AAU). Stories began to leak of a talented big man who had quit swimming to play basketball, but even then only a few schools were interested. Among them was Wake Forest, where Coach Dave Odom badly needed a big post player to complement his main player, point guard Randolph Childress. He had flown to Africa and Europe in search of such a tall post player, so why not the Caribbean?

Odom came out all the way to the Caribbean after

hearing from a former player that Duncan had played then young stud Alonzo Mourning to a draw. However, he was still extremely unsure of what to expect.

Odom's concerns were not allayed when he first arrived at Duncan's house. While Odom talked about the benefits of playing at Wake Forest, Duncan watched a football game and gave utterly no indication that he was paying the slightest bit of attention to Odom. Frustrated, Odom moved his chair right next to the television, and when Duncan still continued to watch the game. Odom asked whether he could turn the TV off, and Duncan responded not by apologizing for his lack of attention, nor by refusing Odom's request, but by repeating everything Odom had said, word for word. To Odom's amazement, he had been paying attention the whole time. Odom offered Duncan a scholarship, but unlike other high school athletes who had made their college decision as early as their junior year, Duncan said that he would wait until the final semester of his senior year before making his decision. After averaging 25 points and 12 rebounds in his final year at St. Dunstan's, Duncan finally made the decision to join Dave Odom and the Wake Forest Demon Deacons.

Chapter 2: College Years at Wake Forest

Freshman Year

Going from the Caribbean to Winston-Salem, North Carolina, was a huge transition for Tim as well as for his future teammates. One teammate went so far as to ask Duncan whether people wore clothes down in the Virgin Islands, while Randolph Childress teased that Duncan had no idea what Washington D.C. was. Dave Odom was so worried about the transition that he considered red-shirting Duncan, but changed his mind when another prospect from Senegal was ruled ineligible.

Despite being surrounded by doubt, Duncan was to start at center, and in the months before the basketball season began, he routinely practiced in an empty gym. One day, Randolph Childress walked into the gym and spotted a near seven-footer dribbling the ball like a guard and taking it coast to coast. Not recognizing his new teammate, Childress ran to Coach Odom's office and told him to get down there and recruit whoever that was in the Wake Forest gym.

Unfortunately, to practice in an empty gym is one thing; to play a game is another. Duncan had to deal with handling the speed and physicality of college ball, and he had the ups and downs which came from being extremely raw at that stage in his career. In his first game against Alaska-Anchorage, Tim Duncan did not even attempt a single shot. In the next game against Hawaii, Duncan grabbed a double-double, and he earned the ACC Player of the Week less than a month into his college career. Later that season against the Clemson Tigers, Duncan was manhandled by opposing center Sharone Wright, who repeatedly dunked over him. Coach Odom called Duncan into his office the next day, and Duncan entered fearing the worst. To Duncan's surprise, Odom struck a soothing tone; having worried that Duncan would lose confidence after such a rough game. Duncan laughed when he realized it, and with a smile on his face, declared "Coach, I'm fine. I'm just having a good time." It was just another sign of Duncan's poise and maturity.

Wake Forest had traditionally been just a stepping stone for superior basketball schools like North Carolina and Duke, but Duncan and Childress changed that. They finished 20-11, won games against both of those schools, and Wake Forest qualified for the NCAA tournament. The Demon Deacons were eliminated in Round two against Kansas, but it had been a good start for Tim Duncan's college career. He had shown off sound post skills as well as incredible defensive instincts, and even as a freshman broke Wake Forest's record for blocked shots in a season.

Sophomore Year

It was in his sophomore year that Duncan really began to develop into not just a good basketball player, but a great one. He had averaged 9.8 points and 9.6 rebounds a game, which was so low only because of the time Duncan needed to adjust. But in his sophomore year, as Wake Forest showcased themselves to be one of the best college teams in the country, Duncan made a huge jump to average 16.8 points and 12.5 rebounds a game. Wake Forest qualified for the NCAA tournament again, and this made it to the Sweet 16. Despite 22 points and eight rebounds from Duncan, Wake Forest was eliminated once again.

The Atlantic Coast Conference (ACC), where Wake Forest was located, had had three players who were viewed as high-level NBA prospects: Joe Smith, Jerry Stackhouse, and Rasheed Wallace. With his great sophomore year, Tim Duncan joined these three as elite NBA prospects and no less an honorary figure than the legendary Jerry West suggested that Duncan would be the #1 pick if he was to enter the 1995 NBA Draft. But while Stackhouse, Smith, and Wallace would enter the NBA, and would all be picked by pick #4, Duncan chose to stay in Wake Forest for another year. He said that he felt that he was too young to join the NBA, though it is possible that he remembered the promise he made to his dying mother to graduate from college.

Junior and Senior Year

In Tim Duncan's junior year, he was forced to carry the burden of leading Wake Forest as his teammate Childress had also declared for the 1995 NBA Draft. Despite playing with inexperienced guards and losing in the NCAA tournament, Duncan won the ACC Player of the Year and Defensive Player of the Year award, improving to average 19.1 and 12.3 rebounds per game. The Demon Deacons made the NCAA tournament, but just as the tournament began, Duncan came down with the flu. He chose to play anyway, and Wake Forest still managed to win their first three games until they ran into Kentucky. The Kentucky Wildcats triple-teamed the ill Duncan and his teammates were unable to take advantage to win the game. After the tournament, Duncan had a momentous decision to make. He would have been the number one pick in the 1996 NBA Draft, a legendary class which included Allen Iverson and Kobe Bryant, and for a time, Duncan seriously considered leaving to join the NBA. After thinking it over for some time, Duncan finally decided to stay for one more year, declaring his desire to win the NCAA tournament. He would once again win the ACC Player of the Year and Defensive Player of the Year award.

Unfortunately, despite the Wake Forest team being a year older, they would fail to win the NCAA tournament in Duncan's senior year, and in fact would be eliminated in just the second round. Duncan's individual numbers would remain impressive as he averaged over 20 points and 14 rebounds per game. He had at this point developed a full-fledged post-game as well as range – he even hit a few three point shots in his senior year! For a third straight year, Duncan won the ACC Player of the Year and Defensive Player of the Year award. Fulfilling his promise to his mother, Duncan would graduate from Wake Forest with honors, earning a Bachelor's in Psychology. There is little doubt that in his subsequent years in the NBA, Duncan used his knowledge of the human mind to both keep himself steady for the big moments where he shined, as well as to outthink his opponents. Or, as NBA athlete Metta World Peace so eloquently put it, "Tim Duncan is gangsta."

Chapter 3: Early Success in the NBA

After graduating from Wake Forest as one of the greatest players in college history, Tim Duncan was the consensus number-one pick in the 1997 NBA Draft. At the draft lottery, the Boston Celtics (15-67) and the Vancouver Grizzlies (14-68) had the best chances of winning the right to select Duncan. However, when the numbers were laid out, it was the San Antonio Spurs with their rookie coach Gregg Popovich who earned the number one pick. This would mark the beginning of the pairing of Duncan and Popovich, who have stuck together for nearly 20 years in the NBA.

The Spurs were not your ordinary team bad enough to get a high lottery pick. Just one year previously in 1995-96 season, they had accumulated a record of 59-23 and had reached the second round of the playoffs behind David "The Admiral" Robinson. But injuries to Robinson, who only played six games in the 1996-97 season, as well as to other key players like Sean Elliott, meant that the Spurs had a much different record of 20-62. This was the season that saw the firing of head coach Bob Hill after he started the year with a record of 3-15. Popovich took over on an interim basis and struggled with a 17-47 record with a depleted San Antonio team.

Yet with the team seemingly recovered, the Spurs were set apart as different from other lottery teams who were just content to wallow in the lottery and collect a few more high picks. San Antonio planned to go right back to being contenders the minute they drafted Duncan. Tim Duncan had no time to waste – he was going to be thrown right into the fire of leading a NBA team with high expectations, and he had to get adjusted to it right away. Thanks to years of leading a team in Wake Forest, it took Duncan no time at all to handle himself in the NBA.

In his first game of the season against the Denver Nuggets on October 31, 1997, Duncan finished with

15 points and 10 rebounds while making six out of nine from the field and three of five from the free throw line in the Spurs' 107-96 win. Granted, Duncan was almost ineffective on the very next night at home during an 83-80 win against the Cleveland Cavaliers on November 1, 1997, a game where Duncan made just four out of seven field goals to score nine points while Robinson led the team with 22 points and nine rebounds. In his third game on November 3, 1997, against the defending champions the Chicago Bulls, Duncan had 19 points and 22 rebounds after making eight out of 14 from the field during their first loss of the season, 87-83.

Duncan and Robinson combined to form a "Twin Towers" frontcourt, a defensive nightmare which prevented opponents from scoring inside. It wouldn't be very long into the season before Duncan would hit the 20-point scoring mark for the first time in his professional career. On November 11, 1997, Duncan would make nine out of 13 from the field and four of six free throws to finish with 22 points and nine rebounds in support of David Robinson's 36 points and 16 rebounds during a very close 93-92 win on the road over the Minnesota Timberwolves. Duncan would hit the 20-point mark in more than half of the games in his rookie season.

He would surpass the 30-point mark for the first time on December 13, 1997, during a home game against the Orlando Magic. He finished with 32 points after making 15 out of 20 from the field and also collected 11 rebounds, 10 of which on defense, during the Spurs' 107-78 win. It would be nearly two months before he reached this mark again, specifically on February 3, 1998, with a 105-96 win on the road visiting the Golden State Warriors. Duncan would convert on 14 out of 25 field goals and six of eight from the foul line to finish with 34 points, 14 rebounds, four assists, three blocked shots and two steals. Duncan would top that scoring performance with a season-high 35 points while also collecting 17 rebounds (11 on defense) and five steals during a 90-83 loss at Golden State on March 4, 1998.

While his offensive numbers and rebounding skills were on display for the Spurs, his defense was a big part of how good he was on defense – especially when defending opposing shot attempts. For example, during the team's 101-86 win over the Boston Celtics on December 26, 1997, Duncan blocked eight shots to go along with 23 points and 15 rebounds (12 of which were collected on the defensive side of the court). He would match that season high on February 28, 1998 during a 100-88 win over the Philadelphia 76ers.

In addition to a lot of his accomplishments, Duncan would be selected to play in the 1998 NBA All-Star Game, quite the accomplishment for any rookie. However, on February 8, 1998 at Madison Square Garden in New York City, Duncan only played about 14 minutes and made just one out of four field goals for two points. He did manage to collect 11 total rebounds (10 of which playing defense) to help the

Western Conference team. They would lose to the Eastern Conference All Stars, 135-114, led by Michael Jordan's 23 points and with Grant Hill scoring an additional 15 points. During the NBA All-Star weekend, Duncan was part of the Shooting Stars competition as part of a trio of Spurs who completed various shots at different angles and distances.

The All-Star Game appearance was just one the honors that Duncan received for his performance as a rookie in the 1997-98 season. He earned a spot on the All-NBA First Team with Karl Malone (Utah Jazz), Shaquille O'Neal (Los Angeles Lakers), Gary Payton (Seattle Super Sonics), and Michael Jordan (Chicago Bulls). He was the first rookie to make the First Team since the legendary Larry Bird in 1980. Duncan was also selected as a member of the league's All-Defensive Second Team and as the winner of the NBA's Rookie of the Year award. This was because the Spurs made a huge jump from winning 20 games in the previous season to 56 games, one of the most impressive turnarounds in NBA history. It was also good enough for second place in the Midwest Division and for the fifth seed in the Western Conference entering the NBA playoffs.

After starting all 82 games in his rookie season, Duncan finished averaging 21.1 points, 11.9 rebounds, nearly three assists and two and a half blocks per game. He was also very good with possession of the ball by turning it over less than four times per game on average. Duncan's offense was highlighted by making 54.9 percent of his total field goal attempts, despite struggling at the foul line with 66.2 percent converted.

Despite the impressive start to Duncan's NBA career, the NBA Playoffs are a completely different animal where legends are made. In Duncan's first playoff game against the Phoenix Suns on April 23, 1998, his legend began with a poor start. He scored just four points in the first half, and Coach Gregg Popovich was forced to bench him. Confident that the rookie was wilting under pressure, Suns coach Danny Ainge decided to focus his defense on Duncan's teammates in the second half. Ainge's tactic proved to be a giant mistake. Duncan erupted for 28 points in the second half, including 10 straight points during the last few minutes of the fourth quarter. Even when Phoenix began to double team, Tim scored in the post again and again, and TNT announcer Marv Albert, his voice growing steadily more crazed, declared "Duncan has gone mad!" In addition to his 32 points, Duncan also grabbed 10 rebounds for the game, securing the 102-96 win. It was an amazing performance by the young rookie.

The Spurs would go on to win against Phoenix in the first round after winning the best-of-five series 3-1 where Duncan converted on 55.7 percent from the field while averaging 20.3 points and almost 10 rebounds. Duncan was also averaging nearly four blocked shots and almost three assists for an overall dominant performance against the Suns.

They would lose in the second round to the Utah Jazz and the best power forward in the league, Karl Malone. Duncan still averaged 21 points and eight rebounds in that series. His highlight game of the series was the first game where he made 13 out of 22 from the field (59.1 percent) and seven of eight free throws to finish with 33 points, 10 rebounds, four blocks and a steal. Overall, Duncan made 49.4 percent from the field and an improved 71.1 percent on the foul line. The Jazz would continue to their second straight NBA Finals matchup against the Chicago Bulls, but it was to be Jordan's sixth title in the 1990s.

It was a tough loss, but the Spurs were just getting started as Duncan was about to become the center of an evolving dynasty in the NBA. Jordan retired and the Bulls were about to move away from their dominance in the NBA which spanned the 1990s. The 1998-99 NBA season would only be 50 games long instead of the usual 82 due to a lockout. With an additional year to work together and build chemistry, the Spurs were better than ever. While they started with a 6-8 record, the Spurs won 37 games, which was the equivalent of winning 60 games in a normal 82-game season, the best record in the entire NBA.

Duncan was finding better efficiency on the court and scoring inside the paint. His highest field goal percentage for a game was on March 16, 1999 after making 13 out of 16 (81.3 percent) and included his first ever completed three-point field goal to finish with 29 points in a 121-109 win visiting the Sacramento Kings. As the season continued and San Antonio continued to build their chemistry, Duncan reached a new personal best in scoring on April 1, 1999 with 39 points after converting on 19 out of 31 field goals to go along with 13 rebounds in a 103-91 win over the Vancouver Grizzlies. His rebounding average didn't feature a 20-rebound game, but he still finished with 37 double-doubles that included 19 rebounds to go with 32 points in a 104-100 loss to the Kings on April 27, 1999.

While he wasn't selected for the 1999 All-Star Game, Duncan would finish with an average of 21.7 points per game and converted on 49.5 percent of his field goals. He also averaged 11.4 rebounds, about two and a half steals and assists throughout his impressive second season in the NBA. Duncan once again made the All-NBA First Team, and San Antonio's defense as well as Tim Duncan's overall polished game got them deep into the playoffs after earning the top seed in the Western Conference.

Duncan and the Spurs would make quick work of the eighth-seeded Minnesota Timberwolves after Duncan averaged just 18.8 points and 10.8 rebounds per game of the first round series. His best overall game of the series was the first game, where he had 26 points and 12 rebounds after making Game 1 on May 9, 1999, with a score of 99-86. In Game 3, Duncan only had 15 points after making just six out of 17 field goals (35.3 percent), but it was a defensive win at 85-71 where he also collected five blocked shots, seven assists, and seven rebounds in the win.

The Spurs would sweep the Los Angeles Lakers who were still trying to develop the chemistry between Kobe Bryant and Shaquille O'Neal. It was in the fourth game of the series where Duncan was on fire as he would make 11 out of 14 field goals (78.6 percent) and just as good of a conversion rate on the foul line while also collecting 14 total rebounds (13 on defense) during a 118-107 win on May 23, 1999. It definitely led the stats to swell for Duncan as he averaged 29 points and nearly 11 rebounds in the series with the Lakers. The numbers weren't as strong in the Western Conference Finals for Duncan with 16.8 points and 9.8 rebounds per game, but the Spurs still swept the Portland Trail Blazers. He had two double-doubles, including a series-best 23 points and 10 rebounds while making eight of 11 field goals (72.7 percent) and seven of 13 free throws in an 86-85 win on May 31,

1999. Duncan blocked five of Portland's shot attempts during the game as well.

San Antonio would continue to ride the momentum all the way to the NBA Finals against the New York Knicks. In the NBA Finals, the biggest stage in all of basketball, Tim Duncan delivered. In the first game of the series on June 16, 1999, Duncan made 13 of 21 field goals (61.9 percent) and seven of 10 free throws to finish with 33 points and 16 rebounds in the 89-77 win in Game 1 to give San Antonio the early 1-0 series lead. The Spurs' defense was strong in Game 2 as they defeated the Knicks 80-67 on June 18, 1999 in a game where Robinson blocked five shots and another four were blocked by Duncan. Duncan also scored 25 points and collected 15 rebounds. While the Knicks would get the Game 3 win at home in Madison Square Garden, 89-81 on June 21, 1999, Duncan bounced back with nine out of 19 field goals (47.4 percent) and 10 of 12 free throws to finish with 28 points and 18 rebounds in the Game 4 win on June 23, 1999 with a score of 96-89.

Throughout the NBA Finals, Duncan averaged more than 27 points per game for the series, as well as 14 total rebounds averaged while converting on 53.7 percent from the field. Those numbers featured his 41 points after making 12 of 22 field goals (54.5 percent) and seven of nine on the foul line during a 78-77 win on June 25, 1999. Duncan almost had a double-double with nine collected on defense. San Antonio defeated New York 4-1 to give the Spurs their first championship. Duncan would receive his first NBA Finals "Most Valuable Player" award. At just 22 years old, Duncan had seemingly already grabbed the crown for best NBA player in the aftermath of Michael Jordan's retirement.

Unfortunately, the next few seasons would be fairly rough for the Spurs when you consider that David Robinson, Sean Elliott, Avery Johnson, and other major players on the 1999 NBA championship team were beginning to enter the twilight of their careers. The Twin Towers who had so thoroughly dominated the NBA defensively now turned into the single Tower, Tim Duncan.

That's because Duncan was very effective for the Spurs' offense. On December 9, 1999, in a home game against the Vancouver Grizzlies, Duncan would reach the 40-point mark for the first time in his career after making 15 out of 22 field goals (68.2 percent) and another 12 of 14 free throws to finish with 42 points in a 99-91 win. Duncan also collected 14 rebounds, four assists, two steals and a blocked shot. A few months later on January 10, 2000, during a 93-86 win over the Utah Jazz, Duncan would top that career high point scoring with 16 of 28 field goals (57.1 percent) and 14 out of 16 from the foul line to have a total of 46 points and 14 rebounds.

In addition to having a higher scoring average which would continue to grow from the first two seasons in the league, Duncan would have a total of 60 double-

doubles in his 74 appearances. He also had his first triple-double on March 25, 2000 during San Antonio's 96-76 win where Duncan finished with 17 points, 17 rebounds and 11 assists. He also collected four blocked shots and a steal on defense. He had two other chances for some unique triple-doubles during that season, including a performance where he scored 23 points, 10 rebounds, and eight blocked shots on November 26, 1999 during a 101-78 rout of the Chicago Bulls. On February 9, 2000, Duncan had eight steals for a near triple-double with 24 points and 13 rebounds during a 106-97 win on the road against the Denver Nuggets.

Duncan would finish the regular season with averages of 23.2 points, 12.4 rebounds, 3.2 assists and 2.2 blocks while making 49 percent of his field goals. Duncan was once again selected to another NBA All-Star Game while also earning a spot on the league's All-NBA First Team and the league's All-Defensive Team. While players like Robinson were starting to show their age, the Spurs still finished with a record of

53-29, enough to put them second in the Midwest Division and fourth in the Western Conference. Near the end of the regular season, Duncan would suffer an injury in his knee's meniscus that kept him out of the first round playoff series against the Phoenix Suns. San Antonio quickly learned how important Duncan was to the team when the older veterans started to show their age.

In Game 1 on April 22, 2000, the Spurs would struggle offensively, shooting just 39.7 percent from the field in a 72-70 loss. Sean Elliot led the team with just 15 points while Robinson made just three of 12 from the field (25 percent) for only 11 points. Robinson would bounce back with 25 points and 15 rebounds during the 85-70 win in the series' second game. He scored 37 points in Game 3 on April 29, 2000, in a 101-94 loss. The Spurs overall shot just 37 percent in an 89-78 loss where the Suns would clinch the first round series, 3-1, on May 2, 2000.

Meanwhile in Los Angeles, a new dynasty had been founded with the combination of Coach Phil Jackson, superstar Shaquille O'Neal, and rising prospect Kobe Bryant. Similar to the 1990s as the head coach of the Chicago Bulls with stars like Michael Jordan and Scottie Pippen, Jackson was able to bring success to Los Angeles by winning three straight NBA championships between 2000 and 2002. While the Spurs were not performing as well in the postseason, they continued to win in the regular season.

Duncan continued to put up more than 20 points, 10 rebounds, and played spectacular defense night in and night out, and additionally, he continued to make the All-NBA First Team. For example, Duncan would play in all 82 games of the 2000-01 season and had 66 double-doubles that included making 15 out of 23 from the field (65.2 percent), six of nine from the foul line (66.7 percent), 36 points and 21 rebounds during a 97-91 win over the Sacramento Kings on January 25, 2001. Later on March 19, 2001, Duncan helped the

Spurs defeat the Portland Trailblazers, 98-85, by finishing with 23 total rebounds – 15 on defense and eight on offense – while also collecting 20 points after making eight out of 19 field goals, and even made a field goal behind the three-point line.

While the Spurs found success in the regular season in 2000-01 with a 58-24 record and the first overall seed in the Western Conference, there were a lot of expectations for Duncan to lead San Antonio to another NBA Finals appearance. In the first game of the Spurs' first round series with the Minnesota Timberwolves on April 21, 2001, Duncan scored 33 points and collected 15 rebounds in an 87-82 win. He was efficient with converting on 13 out of 20 field goals (65 percent) and seven of 10 free throws to go along with four assists and four blocked shots. It was a quick best-of-five series as the Spurs would advance after winning three games to one.

Duncan would explode in the second round series against the in-state rivals, the Dallas Mavericks, with a

4-1 series win where he averaged 27 points, 17.4 rebounds and was shooting about 51 percent from the field. Duncan would start and finish the series with 30-point games, starting with converting 14 out of 22 field goals (63.6 percent) to finish with 31 points and 13 rebounds during the Spurs' 94-78 win on May 5, 2001. A little more than a week later on May 14, 2001, the Spurs clinched the series with a 105-87 win thanks to Duncan scoring 32 points and collecting 20 rebounds after making 12 out of 25 from the field (48 percent) and eight of 11 free throws. He also had five blocked shots, three assists, and one steal in one of those games where he contributed everywhere for the win.

In 2001 and 2002, the Spurs lost both times in the playoffs to the Shaq-Kobe Lakers, including an absolute pounding in 2001 when the Lakers outright swept San Antonio behind 33 points from Kobe Bryant as well as 27 points and 13 rebounds from Shaq for the series. Duncan did his best against the Lakers, but with a declining Robinson and a lack of other great players, it was not enough.

The Spurs would run into a proverbial brick wall formed by the building blocks earlier mentioned in the Los Angeles Lakers. That's because players like Kobe Bryant were stepping up in the Western Conference Finals that began with 45 points in the first game on May 19, 2001, as Los Angles took the early 1-0 series lead by a score of 104-90. While Duncan finished with 28 points and 14 rebounds and received the support of 20 points by Antonio Daniels in that first game, the rest of the team struggled to find an offensive rhythm. Overall, Duncan would average 23 points and 12.3 rebound in the conference finals. The Lakers would sweep the Spurs and win the second consecutive NBA Championship.

The Spurs made some attempts to bounce back the following season with a record of 58-24 to earn the second seed in the Western Conference. Duncan himself would have another All-Star season after he converted on 50.3 percent of his field goals to average career-highs of 25.5 points, 12.7 rebounds, and 3.7 assists as part of earning his first Most Valuable Player Award in 2002. One of the big games came on December 26, 2001 in an exciting 126-123 overtime loss, a game where Duncan made 19 out of 28 from the field (67.9 percent) and all 15 free throw attempts to score a career-high of 53 points while collecting 11 rebounds, four assists, and blocked three shots.

Once again, the Spurs would win a first round best-of-five series in just four games, this time against the Seattle Super Sonics, which included a Game 2 performance where Duncan scored 32 points while collecting 12 rebounds, six blocks, three assists, and one steal on April 22, 2002. Duncan would average about 25.8 points per game in that opening series of the playoffs while also averaging about 11 rebounds, nearly six blocks, and about five and a half assists.

While Duncan was able to continue his individual momentum in the second round with averages of 29 points, 17.2 rebounds, 4.6 assists, and 3.2 blocks, the Spurs would lose to the Lakers who were on their way to winning their third consecutive NBA championship. In the lone win in the second round series with Los Angeles on May 7, 2002, Duncan would finish with 27 points after making 10 out 19 from the field (52.6 percent) and seven of 12 free throws while collecting 17 rebounds, five assists, and five steals. He would have his best games during the last two games of the series that the Lakers won. During an 87-85 loss on May 12, 2002, Duncan scored 30 points after making nine of 15 field goals and 12 of 16 free throws. He also collected 11 rebounds, six assists, and four blocks. While the Lakers clinched the series with a 93-87 win on May 14, 2002, Duncan led the game with 34 points and 25 rebounds (20 of which he collected on defense) while making 11 out of 23 from the field (47.8 percent) and converting on 12 out of 14 free throws.

Chapter 4: The San Antonio Dynasty

Unlike the multiple championships in the 1990s by the Chicago Bulls and in the early 2000s by the Los Angeles Lakers, the San Antonio Spurs didn't win three titles in a row. They were a perennial team despite the playoff exits in the seasons that followed their 1999 NBA Championship in Tim Duncan's second season. They were about to have a run of three championships in a five-year period that would stand as a dynasty in its own right in NBA history.

During the early part of the 2002-03 season, the San Antonio Spurs were looking very strong and had more of the same players leading the way, including Duncan as the big man playing inside the paint. At the same time, the Spurs were also developing some younger players that were beginning to step up their quality of play. San Antonio had a young French point guard named Tony Parker who showed spurts of greatness, as well as an Argentinean star named Manu Ginobili.

Parker needed time to adjust from European-style basketball to the NBA, and the Ginobili was inconsistent. The now 37-year-old David Robinson had also announced that he was going to retire from the NBA at the end of the season. Robinson had deferred to Duncan from the moment the younger of the Twin Towers had arrived, showing the willingness to sacrifice for the team that would define Spurs basketball in the years to come. Now, the Admiral declared that he believed in Duncan, and that Duncan would be able to win another ring in Robinson's final season.

In four of the Spurs' first five games, Duncan had a double-double that included a game where he scored 22 points after making eight out of 17 field goals and six of eight free throws while collecting 15 rebounds in the Spurs' 91-72 win on November 1, 2002. In the very next game visiting the Memphis Grizzlies on November 4, 2002, Duncan made 14 out of 27 field goals (51.9 percent) to finish with 29 points and 14 rebounds, including the game-winning 13-foot field goal with just half a second left, to go along with 14 rebounds, five assists, and two steals during a 103-101 win.

Duncan would continue to put up insane numbers throughout the season, including a season-high 38 points after converting on 16 out of 25 field goals (64 percent) in addition to collecting 16 rebounds, nine assists, and four blocks during a thrilling 108-100 overtime victory on January 14, 2003. Duncan had this performance less than two weeks after scoring 37 points after making 14 out of 18 field goals (77.8 percent) and all nine free throws in a 98-95 win over the Golden State Warriors on January 3, 2003. Duncan would also collect a triple-double on March 14, 2003 during a 107-96 victory over the Los Angeles Clippers where Duncan scored 24 points after making shooting 66.7 percent from the field (10 out of 15) to go along with 15 rebounds and 10 assists.

Near the end of the regular season, the Spurs enjoyed an 11-game winning streak that featured key victories over other Western Conference rivals like the Los Angeles Lakers by a score of 98-89 on March 23, 2003 with Duncan shooting 40 percent from the field (10 out of 25) to score 27 points to go with 17 total rebounds (14 of them collected on defense). Duncan had a number of key contributions in this streak, just like the rest of the season, which included the 92-90 win on the road over the New Orleans Hornets on March 30, 2003 where he made 12 out of 22 field goals, including a three-point basket, to score 33 points while collecting 12 rebounds.

In the Twin Towers' final season, Duncan delivered as the Spurs finished with a record of 60-22 in the 2002-03 season. Duncan wasn't the only reason the Spurs were winning, it could also be attributed to San Antonio being bolstered by the rising play of Parker's 15.5 points per game average, Ginobili's 7.6 points per game, and an elite perimeter defender Bruce Bowen to support Duncan. It was good to have the new and younger talent rise as the veteran Robinson had his worst season in terms of statistics with an average of 8.5 points per game and also averaging about 7.9 rebounds and making about 46.9 percent. It was the first season he failed to average double figures and convert on less than half of his field goal attempts.

With a supporting cast, Duncan won his second straight NBA Most Valuable Player award for the second consecutive season thanks to averaging 23.3 points, 12.9 rebounds, 3.9 assists, and 2.9 steals while making 51.3 percent of his field goals. He also found himself on the All-NBA First Team, the All-Defensive First Team, and with yet another NBA All-Star nomination. San Antonio would have the tiebreaker over the Dallas Mavericks to win the Midwest Division while still collecting the first overall seed in the Western Conference for the NBA Playoffs.

In the first round against the Phoenix Suns, Duncan was more effective on the boards with 23 total rebounds – 20 of which were snagged on defense – with 11 points, six assists and three blocks during San Antonio's 99-86 win in Game 3 on April 25, 2003. While the Suns would tie the series at 2-2, Duncan helped the Spurs jump to a series win with 23 points and 17 rebounds during a 94-82 win on April 29, 2003. He also had a triple-double with 15 points, 20 rebounds, and 10 assists.

San Antonio faced off against the Shaq-and-Kobe duo and the rest of the Lakers for the third straight year. While the Spurs were a team that rallied around Duncan and Robinson, the Lakers were beset by the Shaq-Kobe feud over who was the more dominant player, which made it hard for the Lakers to function as a team overall. For example, Game 2 featured Bryant and O'Neal each scoring 27 points while the other three starters combined for 13 points. While Duncan scored just 12 points and 13 rebounds, the Spurs were led by Bruce Bowen's 27 points and Manu Ginobili's 17 points for the 114-95 win on May 7,

2003. The Spurs would eventually win the second round series, 4-2, after their 110-82 victory in Game 6 on May 15, 2003 where Duncan converted 64 percent of his field goals (16 out of 25) to score 37 points, 16 rebounds, four assists, and two blocks.

The Spurs beat the Dallas Mavericks and their great power forward, Dirk Nowitzki, in the Western Conference Finals where Duncan would average 28 points and 16.7 rebounds while making 56.9 percent of his field goals, and they would win after six games. After being matched up with the New Jersey Nets in the NBA Finals, Duncan would make an immediate impact by making 11 out of 17 field goals (64.7 percent) and 10 of 14 free throws to score 32 points to go along with 20 rebounds, seven blocked shots, six assists and three steals during the Game 1 win, 101-89, on June 4, 2003. Duncan had at least a double-double in every game of the series. He would have a triple-double with another 20-rebound game during Game 6 on June 15, 2003, in an 88-77 win where he also

49

scored 21 points, collecting 10 assists and eight blocks. His Twin Tower counterpart had a strong double-double in his final NBA game with 13 points and 17 rebounds. The Spurs won their second title, and Duncan was once again named Finals MVP. True to his promise, David Robinson retired afterwards.

With Robinson gone, the Lakers presented themselves as even more formidable opponents with the additions of Gary Payton and Karl Malone. The Spurs picked up Robert Horry in an effort to replace Robinson, and Ginobili and Parker continued to improve. Duncan was also a little hesitant to enter the leader role for the team, even though he had been a big part of the Spurs winning two championships in his time with the team, and at this point and he would eventually fill in the void left when Robinson retired from the NBA.

In the first season (2003-04) for the Spurs without Robinson, Duncan found quick success on October 29, 2003 at the Pepsi Center in Denver, Colorado. Duncan struggled in shooting with 31.8 percent from the field (seven out of 22) to score just 17 points, but he would also finish with 21 total rebounds (16 on defense, five on offense) and blocked eight shots by opposing shooters, granted the Nuggets would still win 80-72. There were better games ahead for the Spurs and for Duncan. For example, on December 5, 2003, he made 19 out of 34 field goals (55.9 percent) and nine of 13 free throws to score the season-high mark of 47 points while collecting 12 rebounds during a 105-94 win over the Orlando Magic.

While the Minnesota Timberwolves power forward Kevin Garnett would win the 2004 MVP award, Duncan still managed to make the All-NBA First Team after he finished with averages of 22.3 points, 12.4 rebounds, and converted on about 50.1 percent of his total field goal attempts for the season, all while playing just 69 games on the season due to minor injuries. It was another good season where the Spurs finished with a record of 57-25, which was good for the third seed in the Western Conference.

In the first round of the 2004 NBA Playoffs, Duncan would average about 24.3 points and 10 rebounds during the four-game sweep of the Memphis Grizzlies, which included a Game 2 performance on April 19, 2004 in an 87-70 win where Duncan made eight out of 14 field goals (57.1 percent) and seven of 14 free throws to have 23 points, 12 rebounds, five blocks and three assists, while Parker would lead the team with 27 points and seven assists, with another 14 points from veteran Robert Horry as he came off the bench.

Unfortunately, the Spurs would find themselves facing their familiar foes from Los Angeles, and the Lakers had built quite a team of their own to improve themselves. The Spurs had a good start to the series to jump ahead 2-0 as Duncan was extremely effective shooting in Game 1 with 13 of 18 from the field (72.2 percent) to score 30 points while also collecting 11 rebounds. San Antonio would win the second game of the series on May 5, 2004 with a score of 95-85 at home. Duncan would score 24 points and collect seven rebounds, and his teammate Parker would led all Spurs with 30 points. Duncan also converted on seven out of 13 field goals (53.8 percent) and 10 out from the foul line.

Unfortunately, Duncan was not able to continue that momentum into Game 3 where he made just 28.6 percent of his field goals and scored 10 points in a 105-81 loss on May 9, 2004. Game 4 wasn't much better as Duncan made 38.9 percent, although he did make two out of five behind the three-point line to score 19 points to go along with 10 rebounds and eight assists in the 98-90 loss on May 11, 2004. Duncan did his best to keep the Spurs close in a critical Game 5, including hitting an incredibly difficult fade-away jumper over Shaq and Malone to put the Spurs ahead by one point with 0.4 seconds left. Everyone thought the game was over but then in one of the greatest shots in NBA history, Lakers point guard Derek Fisher hit a miracle buzzer beater to win the game 74-73 on May 13, 2004. San Antonio did not manage to recover from the devastating loss and were eliminated in the very next game, 88-76, on May 15, 2004. Duncan was the only starter to score in double figures with 20 points while Ginobili (16), Devin Brown (15) and Horry (12) contributed as reservists coming off of the bench. The Lakers would move on to the NBA Finals only to lose to the Detroit Pistons in five games.

As the 2004-05 season began, the amount of assistance given to Tim Duncan improved dramatically. While Tony Parker and Manu Ginobili had been useful role players over the past two years, they now became stars in their own rights, complimenting Duncan's defense with their offensive prowess. Ginobili made the 2005 All-Star team that year, and Bruce Bowen made the All-Defensive team.

Duncan was still getting plenty of points and almost as many rebounds with a total of 44 double-doubles and averaging 20.3 points per game during his 66 appearances. He also converted about 49.6 percent of his attempted field goals while also averaging 11.1

rebounds, 2.7 assists, and 2.6 blocked shots. While players like Parker, Ginobili and Bowen were stepping up, Duncan was still one of the league's most effective big men. One of his best offensive performances was during a 102-96 loss at home to the Seattle Super Sonics on December 8, 2004, where he made 14 out of 24 from the field (58.3 percent) and another 10 of 14 free throws for 39 points, 10 rebounds, and 4 blocks. Not long after that on December 11, 2004, Duncan would score another 34 points after making an amazing 13 out of 15 from the field (86.7 percent) and an additional eight of 10 free throws in a 116-97 victory over the Cleveland Cavaliers.

And while his scoring was still above the 20-point-average mark, he was still collecting plenty of rebounds on both the offensive and defensive sides of the court. There were two separate games where Duncan collected 19 rebounds. The first was on January 21, 2005 in a close 128-123 win at Phoenix where Duncan also scored another 30 points and made

60 percent from the field; the second was in a close 84-82 loss to Memphis on February 26, 2005 where his 19 rebounds went with 27 points and an even 50 percent on his field goals.

San Antonio would have another successful season with a record of 59-23, the Southwest Division crown, and the second seed in the Western Conference for the NBA Playoffs, which earned them a first round matchup with the Denver Nuggets. The Spurs would lose the first game on April 24, 2005 with Duncan only making seven out of 22 field goals to score 18 points in a 93-87 defeat. The Spurs took the next four games to clinch the first round series. Duncan's best game was in Game 4 after making 13 of 23 field goals and 13 of 14 from the foul line to score 39 points and 14 rebounds as the Spurs defeated the Nuggets, 126-115.

That momentum carried over into the second round against the Seattle Super Sonics where the Spurs defeated them in the first game on May 8, 2005 by a score of 103-81. Parker led the team with 29 points after making 11 of 18 from the field while Duncan had 22 points, nine rebounds, five assists and four blocks. It was much of the same during Game 2 on May 10, 2005 during a 108-91 win where Duncan had 25 points as one of three players to score more than 20 points – Ginobili led the team with 28 points and Parker also contributed 22 of his own. Seattle wasn't a team to slack off in the playoffs as they would tie the series at 2-2 after winning Games 3 and 4 at the Key Arena in Seattle. The team was led by Ray Allen, who was known for making plenty of three-point field goals, and also featured Rashard Lewis and Luke Ridnour. San Antonio would not be denied an opportunity to play for the Western Conference Finals as they defeated Seattle 103-90 in Game 5 on May 17, 2005 where Duncan scored 20 points and had 14 rebounds, although Ginobili was the real star with 39 points to give the Spurs the 3-2 lead. Duncan would get the game-winning field goal from just a few feet away with just half a second left in Game 6 on May 19, 2005 as San Antonio took the 98-96 win in Seattle. The series-winning basket were two of Duncan's 26 points that didn't come easy as he made a mere 28.6 from the field and had 14 of 17 free throws.

The Spurs advanced through the playoffs and found themselves facing another familiar foe, the Phoenix Suns, for the conference finals. In the first game, Duncan made 10 of 21 from the field (47.6 percent) for a total of 28 points and had 15 rebounds during a 121-114 win on May 22, 2005. Duncan followed that up during the second game on May 24, 2005 in a 110-108 win over the Suns. His 30 points came from making 10 of 19 from the field (52.6 percent) and another 10 of 11 free throws. The third game would be another great performance from Duncan as he led the team with 33 points and 15 rebounds after making 52.9 percent from the field and all 15 on the foul line as the Spurs would finish on a 3-0 series lead with the 102-92 win on May 28, 2005. While the Suns would get a win in Game 4, Duncan would get another 31 points and 15 rebounds after making a 58.3 percent (14 of 24) from the field in a 101-95 win at the American West Arena in Phoenix. After a tough Western Conference victory over the Phoenix Suns, where Suns coach Mike D'Antoni declared Duncan "the best player in the game," they made the NBA Finals for a third time.

San Antonio challenged the defending champions the Detroit Pistons, who had surprised and humiliated the Lakers team which had beaten the Spurs last year. Both teams emphasized defense and many NBA fans were turned off by the gritty, tough, low-scoring games. Tim Duncan could not have cared less about that. On June 9, 2005, the Spurs defense held the Pistons to less than 70 points during an 84-69 win. Detroit only made 38.3 percent of their field goals as a team. On the other side of the court, Ginobili led San Antonio with 26 points while Duncan had 24 points and 17 rebounds of his own. The Spurs would have similar success at home in the second game on June 12, 2005 with a 97-76 win over the Pistons. Duncan didn't need to shoot much with five of 10 field goals and eight of nine free throws to finish with 18 points and 11 rebounds while Ginobili led the team again with 27 points after making 75 percent from the field.

The Pistons refused to be swept and would not relinquish their championship so easily. In Game 3 on June 14, 2005, at the Palace of Auburn Hills in Michigan, Duncan would make just five out of 15 shots for 14 points and 10 rebounds as San Antonio made just 43.3 percent leading the Pistons to the win, 96-79. The Pistons followed that up with a dominant 102-71 win to tie the series 2-2 on June 16, 2005. Duncan was five of 17 from the field (29.4 percent) to finish with just 16 points and had just as many rebounds. He would rebound quickly – literally – in Game 5 on June 19, 2005 with a 96-95 win led by Duncan's 26 points and 19 rebounds after making 11 out of 24 from the field (45.8 percent).

After the Pistons tied the series up at the Spurs' home court on June 21, 2005 with a 95-86 win, San Antonio would have a defensive dogfight in the seventh game of the series for the 81-74 win on June 23, 2005. Duncan led the team all players with 25 points and 11 rebounds, with Ginobili scoring 23 points of his own. During the seven games, Duncan averaged 20.6 points, 14.1 rebounds and made 41.9 percent of his field goals to help San Antonio win another championship and begin Duncan's third reign as the NBA Finals MVP honor.

It was in 2005-06 that a recurring theme began to pop up like clockwork every NBA season, only to be swatted down by the San Antonio machine. It was one which claimed that the San Antonio Spurs were old and on the decline. Duncan was only 29 that season, but he battled with a severe case of plantar fasciitis, an injury of one's heel, for most of the season. While he still played 80 games that season, his effectiveness was limited. He posted career lows in points (18.6) and rebounds (11.0) and for the first time in his career, failed to make the All-NBA First Team.

The team was still coming together for a very good season where Duncan still had 52 double-doubles. One of those was on December 7, 2005 when the Spurs defeated the Miami Heat by a score of 98-84 in Texas. Duncan made 28 points after making 11 of 18 from the field (61.1 percent) along with 16 rebounds, four blocks, three assists and three steals. Less than a week later on December 13, 2005, Duncan made 12 of 25 field goals (48 percent) to score 27 points while collecting 22 total rebounds (18 of them collected on defense) to help the Spurs get a decisive 95-87 win over the Los Angeles Clippers. The only other game where Duncan was close to hitting the difficult 20-rebound mark was on November 21, 2005, during a 96-93 win on the road against the Sacramento Kings. Duncan had 22 points and 19 rebounds to go along with four assists and four steals.

Despite all of the struggles with Duncan's heel, he would fully recover in time for the playoffs where the Spurs would finish with a 63-19 record and another

Southwest Division banner to hang in the AT&T Center. This would give San Antonio the first overall seed in the Western Conference. The Spurs came out strong with a 122-88 win in Game 1 of their first round series with the Sacramento Kings on April 22, 2006. Duncan was limited to six field goal attempts and finished with 11 points, but Parker led the team with 25 points and Nazr Mohammed had another 18 points. He also only shot four of 10 for 14 points and 13 rebounds during the second game on April 25, 2006 where the Spurs won 128-119. The Kings would take Games 3 and 4 at their home court in California, but Duncan's involvement would continue to grow, and that included his 24 points and nine rebounds during the Game 5 win on May 2, 2006, 109-98. The Spurs would then follow that up with a 105-83 win on May 5, 2006, to clinch the series. Parker led the team with 31 points while Duncan only had to shoot six of eight from the field for 15 points.

San Antonio had made it to the Western Conference Semifinals against the Dallas Mavericks. This series was an exciting, tightly contested one, and was nominated in 2010 by TNT to be one of the best playoff series of the decade, spanning the length of all scheduled seven games.

Duncan had a strong game in the opening contest on May 7, 2006, in an 87-85 victory after making 12 of 24 field goals and seven of 12 free throws to finish with 31 points, 13 rebounds, four assists, and two blocks. The Mavericks would take the next three games where Duncan did everything he could offensively by averaging 31.3 points during that losing streak (he also converted on 62.5 percent of his field goal attempts). On May 17, 2006, during Game 5 of the series, Duncan would make 13 of 19 field goals (68.4 percent) and 10 of 15 on the foul line to finish with 36 points and 12 rebounds during a 98-97 win. This was followed by a 91-86 win on May 19, 2006 where Duncan struggled with eight of 21 field goals for 24 points, leaving Ginobili to lead the team again with 30 points and 10 rebounds. While Duncan had 41 points and 15 rebounds after making 12 out of 24 from the field and 17 of 23 from the foul line in the key Game 7, a bad foul by Manu Ginobili against Dirk Nowitzki in the final seconds proved decisive. The Mavericks won the game on May 22, 2006 with a score of 119-111 which would also give Dallas the series. This would continue to the NBA Finals where they lost to Dwayne Wade, Shaquille O'Neal, and the rest of the Miami Heat in only six games.

2006-07 Season – Championship

The next NBA season showed yet another great example of Tim Duncan's commitment to the team over his individual glory. With his body fully recovered, Duncan returned to the All-NBA First Team and scored 20 points a game, had 10.6 rebounds per game, and was able to make 54.6 percent of his field goals, which was close to his rookie season's 54.9

percent career high mark. Not bad for someone who would turn the age of 30 during that season, right?

One of his early highlights was on November 19, 2006 where Duncan made 13 of 17 from the field goals and nine of 11 free throws to finish with 35 points and 14 rebounds during the Spurs' 108-99 victory on the road over the Sacramento Kings. It was a tough loss where the Spurs were unable to defend their NBA Championship. It was one of Duncan's 45 double-doubles throughout the season and he nearly had two triple-doubles to add onto that in late January.

On January 26, 2007, Duncan had an impressive overall game with 10 of 16 field goals and six of 10 free throws to finish with 26 points to go along with 13 rebounds and blocked nine opposing shots during a 112-96 victory over the Memphis Grizzlies. Two days later on January 28, 2007, during a 96-94 win on the road against the Los Angeles Lakers, Duncan scored another 31 points, collected another 14 rebounds and had nine assists. He also had three blocks in that game as well. These games were shortly after a performance where he made a season-high 15 field goals to make 53.6 percent of his shots, scored 37 points, and collected 10 rebounds, four assists, and a block on January 24, 2007 in a 90-85 loss to the Houston Rockets.

However, it was still one of his most efficient seasons in terms of shooting from the field. He had a perfect field goal percentage back on December 20, 2006 where he made all eight field goals to score 21 points in a 105-98 win over the Memphis Grizzlies. That carried over towards the end of the regular season with 11 of 14 from the field (78.6 percent) and four of nine free throws to finish with 26 points, 13 rebounds, four assists, four blocks, and two steals during a 109-100 win on April 11, 2007.

The Spurs wouldn't win their Southwest Division, finishing 58-24 on the season. The team that eliminated them from the playoffs in the prior season, the Dallas Mavericks, were atop both the division and the Western Conference after winning 67 games that season. There were a lot of expectations that the Mavericks would have another strong run that would possibly lead to another appearance in the NBA Finals. However, when the eighth-seeded Golden State Warriors (42-40 in the regular season) shocked the world by upsetting the Dallas Mavericks in the first round, the road to a championship and yet another Finals MVP award appeared wide open for the Spurs.

While Dallas struggled with Golden State, the Spurs would take care of the Denver Nuggets rather easily in just five games. While the Nuggets won the first game 95-89, Duncan bounced back on April 25, 2007 with a 97-88 victory. Duncan made nine of 17 field goals and four of six free throws to finish with 22 points. Parker also had 20 points, while Ginobili had 17 points. Duncan's shooting efficiency would improve throughout the series to Game 5 where he would make 52.6 percent of his field goals (10 of 19) in a game where he finished with 23 points, 12 rebounds, and five assists in a 93-78 win on May 2, 2007.

San Antonio would then find themselves having to face the tougher Phoenix Suns in the second round, which sent the series to six games where Duncan averaged an insane 26.8 points per game while collecting an average of 13.7 rebounds and made about 57.3 percent of his shots in that round of the playoffs. In the first game of the series on May 6, 2007, Duncan made 12 of 24 field goals and nine of 15 from the foul line to finish with 33 points while collecting 16 rebounds and three blocks in a 111-106 win. About a week later on May 12, 2007, Duncan helped give San Antonio a 2-1 series with a 108-101 win that featured Duncan making 12 of 19 field goals (63.2 percent) in a 33-point game; he also collected 19 rebounds and three blocks in that game as well.

The Spurs would win the series 4-2 to advance to the Western Conference Finals where they would face the Phoenix Suns. Duncan averaged 21.8 points and 9.6

rebounds as San Antonio would win the series in five games. While Duncan wasn't at his best in the Game 4 win, 91-79 on May 28, 2007, with six of 13 field goals and seven of 12 free throws to finish with 19 points, Ginobili led the team with 22 points. The Spurs would close out the series with a 109-84 win in Game 5 on May 30, 2007. Duncan and Parker each scored 21 points and also received help from Ginobili's 12 points.

The Spurs would eventually take on LeBron James and the Cleveland Cavaliers in the NBA Finals. Coached by defensive guru Mike Brown, the Cavaliers completely planned to shut down Duncan with players like Anderson Varejao and Žydrūnas Ilgauskas. While Duncan struggled against this tough defensive scheme, the focus on Duncan meant that his teammates were free to do as they wished, and Tony Parker in particular took advantage of this opportunity. Tony Parker averaged 26 points per game for the series. In the first game on June 7, 2007, Parker led the team with 27 points and seven rebounds while Duncan made 58.8 percent from the field (10 of 17) while also collecting 13 rebounds, five blocks, and two steals on defense. On June 10, 2007, the Spurs would get another win by a score of 103-92 where Parker would lead the team with 30 points after making 13 of 20 field goals, followed by Ginobili's 25 points after making four of six from behind the three-point line and Duncan making 23 points that went with nine total points and eight assists. However, the third game would be a defensive struggle where the Spurs were able to pull out a 75-72 victory. Parker led the team with 17 points and there were 14 points from Duncan that were joined with nine rebounds, three assists, two blocks and one steal on June 12, 2007. The Spurs would close out the four-game sweep with an 83-82 win in Cleveland, granted they held off a late Cleveland rush with Damon Jones hitting a three-point field goal to bring the score to within the one-point final differential. Duncan struggled to score 12 points after making four of 15 field goals (26.7 percent) while Ginobili led the team with 27 points while Parker had 24 points of his own.

The Spurs swept the Cavaliers and won their fourth title. However, even though Duncan's defense had limited LeBron to shoot just 36 percent for the series and had thus given Parker the chance to score at will, Parker was the one to receive the Finals MVP award. Many other NBA superstars would have been irate to see such a prestigious award handed to a lesser teammate, but no one was happier for Parker than Duncan, who admitted that his own personal play had been sub-par. With his fourth title in eight years, many experts overwhelmingly acclaimed Duncan to be the greatest power forward in the history of the NBA.

Chapter 5: Playoff Disappointments

While the Spurs continued to remain one of the top teams in the NBA over the next few years, they were continually disappointed in their search to secure a fifth title. While Duncan, Parker, and Ginobili still remained excellent players in their own rights, Bruce Bowen began to decline and the Spurs lacked good teammates around the main three players, especially at the crucial center position. In 2008, the Spurs won 56 games and made the Western Conference Finals against the Los Angeles Lakers. While many had predicted a close, hard-fought series, the Spurs were dispatched in just five games as Duncan struggled to contain new Lakers big man, Pau Gasol. In 2009, the Spurs lost in the first round against the Dallas Mavericks. It was the first time Tim Duncan had been eliminated in the first round. In 2010, the Spurs won 50 games, the lowest win total of Duncan's career. The Spurs would beat the Dallas Mavericks in the first round and avenge the previous year's defeat, but the Phoenix Suns would in turn avenge their losses in 2005 and 2007 as they swept the Spurs in four games.

Many people, such as national sports columnist Bill Simmons, were convinced that such a shocking defeat meant the end of the Spurs dynasty, but over the 2010-11 season, San Antonio seemed to prove them wrong. Tim Duncan paced himself, playing below 30 minutes per game for the first time in his career while also averaging a career low in points and rebounds per game. While he failed to make the All-NBA Team for the first time in his career, Duncan and Parker led San Antonio to win 61 games in 2011. Then the Spurs were upset in the first round by the rising Memphis Grizzlies, who were led by Mike Conley, Zach Randolph, and Rudy Gay. Duncan in particular struggled to contain Memphis power forward Zach Randolph, who bullied his way into the paint again and again. Was this the end? Duncan had been so consistent year after year, night after night as he attempted to lead the Spurs. Now, at the age of 34, having lost in the first round as the #1 seed, was this the end of the storied career of Tim Duncan?

In a sense, it was. The days of Tim Duncan singlehandedly guiding San Antonio to victory as he had done in the 2003 Finals were over. Unlike so many other legendary players who stuck around in the NBA years after they had declined and refused to take a smaller role, Duncan accepted becoming just one piece of the San Antonio Spurs – an elite piece, but just a piece nonetheless. Rather than focusing their team around Duncan, the 2011-12 Spurs had a balanced attack, as eight rotation players averaged over 8 points per game. Under Coach Gregg Popovich's leadership, the Spurs also redefined themselves, moving from a stout defensive team dependent on Duncan to clog the paint, to an offensive team with great spacing and ball movement that now depending more on Duncan's passing. The balanced attack meant fewer opportunities for Duncan to score, and he failed to make the All-Star team for the first time in his career. Nevertheless, the Spurs once again finished atop the Western Conference, and even won 50 games despite a lockout shortening the season to 66 games. San Antonio finished the season on a roll, winning their final 12 games. In the playoffs, the Spurs continued the streak and won their first 10 games, sweeping both the Utah Jazz and the Los Angeles Clippers as well as winning the first two games against the Oklahoma City Thunder in the Western Conference Finals. Afterwards, Oklahoma City's trio of stars, James Harden, Russell Westbrook, and Kevin Durant, began to hit jumper after jumper, and the offensive onslaught proved to be too much. The Spurs lost the next four games, and their season was over.

In the offseason, Duncan got down to work. The NBA had changed over the past several years. Elite big men had used to dominate the league, but with a new emphasis on small-ball and perimeter play, he had to adjust. Duncan entered the 2012 training camp 20 pounds lighter, and now moved faster than ever before, even at the age of 36. The Spurs won 58 games, and after missing the All-Star Team last year, Duncan jumped back up to make the All-NBA First Team for the 10th time in his career. Only Kobe Bryant and Kareem Abdul-Jabbar have made the First Team more than 10 times. The Oklahoma City Thunder traded James Harden at the beginning of the 2012-13 season, and Russell Westbrook tore his meniscus at the beginning of the playoffs. Taking advantage of this timing, the Spurs cruised through the first three rounds of the playoff, avenging their 2011 defeat to the Grizzlies by sweeping them. Duncan would rematch with LeBron James, now on the Miami Heat with Dwayne Wade and Chris Bosh, in the NBA Finals once again.

In the first few games of the series, Duncan played within the team, content with watching Tony Parker and wingman Danny Green keep pace with the Miami Heat. As the series progressed, and Miami's lack of reliable big men defenders became more apparent, Duncan began to take on a more assertive role. The Spurs led 3-2 going into the crucial Game 6, and in the first half, the 37-year old Duncan repeatedly outhustled the younger All-Star forward Chris Bosh, scoring 25 points. Duncan finished with 30 points and 17 rebounds, but in one of the oddest coaching moves of the series, Gregg Popovich chose to put Duncan on the bench in the final minute of the game. Duncan watched helplessly as the team, without their primary big man, gave up offensive rebounds on two straight possessions, which led to three-point shots by LeBron James and Ray Allen. Miami would go on to win Game 6 103-100. In Game 7, Duncan had 24 points and 12 rebounds, but missed a crucial layup, and the Miami Heat won the series. The Spurs were as close as any team has ever been to winning a championship without actually obtaining it – so much so that in Game 6, the arena security made initial preparations to bring the championship trophy out on the floor before the Heat tied the game. Many believed that the Spurs simply could not recover from such a devastating loss, as the stoic Duncan was on the verge of tears in the postgame press conference. Duncan said to reporters:

"To be at this point with this team in a situation where people kind of counted us out, is a great accomplishment to be in a Game 7, or to be in a Game 6 up one and two chances to win an NBA championship and not do it, that's tough to swallow."

That fifth title was more important to Duncan than to anyone else in the team because it would have cemented his status as the best superstar in his era. Only Kobe Bryant had won five among his peers, but if Duncan were to win a fifth at this stage of his career, he would have won one title in each of the last three decades, which no one has ever done. As close as he was, 28 seconds away from it to be exact in Game 6, it wasn't meant to be for the Spurs and for Duncan, at least not for that season. Instead of sulking in defeat, the San Antonio Spurs entered the 2013-14 season with the title in mind rather than vengeance for the Miami Heat. The 2014 Spurs featured a record 10 international players on their roster and the reason was simple: to play team basketball as it is played on the international level. Gregg Popovich had engineered a formula where he managed the minutes of his starters during the regular season by expanding his rotation. So with the 10 international players in his squad, The Spurs not only had a deep rotation, they also had a handful of international guys who could shoot the rock from the outside while running an offense anchored on passing and ball movement.

The Spurs' Big Three, Tim Duncan, Manu Ginobili and Tony Parker were also hounded by injuries and were getting older. In order for the Spurs to return to the NBA Finals, they would need their three superstars to be fresh and healthy once the playoffs arrived.

Chapter 6: Return to the Championship

The Spurs started the 2013-2014 season like a team on a serious mission of redemption, winning 11 straight games from November 5 to November 26, 2013 en route to a very impressive 13-1 start. Duncan himself had one of the statistically lowest producing months of his career in November 2013, averaging just 13.1 points and 7.3 rebounds per game. In his first game of the season, Duncan only played 17 minutes and made just one out of six field goals (16.7 percent) and just one of three free throws to finish with what was close to a career-low of three points on October 30, 2013 in a 101-94 win over the Memphis Grizzlies.

Duncan would return with a decent game after taking a brief break on November 2, 2013 visiting the Portland Trail Blazers. Despite the 115-105 loss, Parker would convert on 52.2 percent from the field (12 of 23) to score 24 points while collecting seven rebounds and one assist. The month remained tough for Duncan and he had one of his worst career games on November 13, 2013 during a game with the Washington Wizards. Duncan made just one out of 12 field goals for his lowest percentage (8.3 percent) and had just two points and eight rebounds while the Spurs would win 92-79. Parker led the team with 16 points, followed by Boris Diaw's 15 points off the bench.

Duncan got better as the season progressed. On December 2, 2013 Duncan became the oldest player in NBA history to record a 20-20 game with 23 points and 21 rebounds in a 102-100 win over the Atlanta Hawks. Duncan punctuated that record by hitting the game-winning jump shot with four tenths of a second left to play. Duncan would average 16.1 points per game for the month of December, and his rebounding increased as well with almost 12 rebounds per game. He also had a higher field goal percentage (48.4 percent) than the opening month of the 2013-14 season. Nearly two weeks later, Duncan had a near triple-double on December 13, 2013 where he had 12 points, 14 rebounds and eight assists during a 117-110 win against the Minnesota Timberwolves. The Spurs were carried by Parker scoring 29 points and Ginobili scoring another 20 points off of the bench.

January was still tough, but he kept having a few good games here and there, but the team remained competitive considering they had stars in Ginobili and Parker stepping up when the 38-year-old Duncan was not playing at his best. His best game in the new month of 2014 was during a 110-108 win on the road against the Memphis Grizzlies on January 7, 2014. He made nine of 16 (56.3 percent) from the field and six of eight on the foul line to score 24 points to go along with 17 rebounds, four assists, two blocks, and one steal. This was one of the Spurs' best games overall as the team shot 51.8 percent and saw a new stars emerging with Marco Belinelli scoring 19 points and Kawhi Leonard scoring 17 points.

February was Duncan's best month of the season because he averaged 18.9 points and 10.7 rebounds and a season-most 31 minutes per game in 10 games for the month. On February 5, 2014, during a road match against the Washington Wizards in the nation's capital, Duncan made 13 of 20 field goals (65 percent) to finish with 31 points to help the Spurs defeat the Wizards 125-118. He also had 11 rebounds, five assists, three blocks and two steals on defense. In the final game of the month on February 28, 2014, Duncan made 50 percent from the field to finish with 17 points, 16 rebounds and six assists as he led San Antonio to a 92-82 win at home.

However, the breakout performance in February wasn't enough to make a case for the 2014 Western Conference All-Star team. Along with Mike Conley, DeMarcus Cousins, Anthony Davis, and Goran Dragic, Duncan was among the snubs when the West's reserves were named. It was only the third time in Duncan's career that he missed the All-Star bus. That was expected since Duncan was playing the fewest minutes per game of his career.

The Spurs started to separate themselves from the rest of the league after the All-Star Break as they started an incredible winning streak after losing on February 21. By March 10, the Spurs had taken over the best record in the NBA at 46-16 after six straight wins as the Spurs took a one-half game over their rivals the Oklahoma City Thunder.

On March 16, 2014, Tim Duncan made seven of 10 field goals to score 16 points and six rebounds to help the Spurs win their 10th consecutive game in a 122-104 win over the Utah Jazz, becoming the first team in the 2014 season to win 50 games. In doing so, the Spurs also extended their league-best record of consecutive seasons with at least 50 wins to 15 seasons. The current win streak was also the Spurs' second double-digit winning streak of the season after winning 11 consecutive games in November. The Spurs were not yet done. Later that month on March 26, 2014 at home against the Denver Nuggets, Duncan had another quality game, making 12 of 20 from the field (60 percent) to score 29 points while collecting 13 rebounds, five assists, and two steals to help the Spurs defeat Denver, 108-103.

On April 3, 2014, the Spurs beat the Golden State Warriors 111-90 to extend their franchise longest winning streak to 19 games. Duncan shot seven out of 11 from the field, including six out of seven in the first half, mostly bank shots and mid- range jumpers, scoring 15 points. The team was led by Parker, again, who had 18 points. The 18-game record winning streak would fall in their next game as the Spurs would lose to the Thunder in their next game, 106-94 on April 3, 2014. Duncan struggled with five of 15 made field goals (33.3 percent) and seven of eight on the foul line to finish with 17 points, but it was Patrick Mills as the star of the game with 21 points to lead the team.

It was clear that Popovich's strategy to restrict Duncan's minutes was paying off because Duncan was producing better numbers than he was at the start of the season. His outside shooting, too, began to improve as compared to the previous months. This made the Spurs only more dangerous. Near the end of the season on April 10, 2014, Duncan would score 20 points after making seven of 12 from the field (58.3 percent) while collecting 15 rebounds to help the Spurs beat the Dallas Mavericks on the road, 109-100.

A couple of weeks later, Duncan and Manu Ginobili sat out the second of a back-to-back to rest and watched Danny Green set a career high 33 points as the Spurs came back from 21 points down to defeat the Phoenix Suns 112-104 and improve to 68-18 on the season. With the victory, the Spurs clinched home court advantage throughout the playoffs and set the tone for what would be a dominating playoff campaign. Coach Gregg Popovich had said all year long that getting the best record wasn't their priority, but the moment they had a shot at it, they added an insurance policy which would become crucial in the playoffs.

The Spurs completed an incredible regular season where they became the first team since the ABA merger not to have a single player average 30 minutes or more per game. The Spurs' starters also missed a combined 75 games during the regular season and Popovich had to manufacture 30 different starting line-ups with 17 different starters as a result. Throughout the injuries, there was one constant: Tim Duncan. The Big Fundamental played in a total of 74 games, his most since suiting up for 76 of them during the 2010-2011 season. Perhaps more stunning than any of those accomplishments was the fact that it was 17-year veteran Tim Duncan who played the most minutes across the team all season long. Duncan's 2,158 total minutes was 142 more than the second most played Spur, Marco Belinelli. Forget the fact that Duncan's 15.1 points and 9.7 rebounds per game were both the second lowest of his storied career.

It wasn't about the statistics as much as it was about the pacing and how fresh Duncan looked just before the playoffs began. All of the above-mentioned numbers were a big reason why San Antonio would finish with a record of 62-20 and first in the Southwest Division. This also earned the Spurs the first overall seed in the Western Conference, just one game above the second-seeded Oklahoma City Thunder (59-23).

The Spurs opened their title bid against Dirk Nowitzki and the Dallas Mavericks. After getting dominated by the Spurs' three point shooting and bench scoring during their regular season meetings, the Dallas Mavericks limited the Spurs to 3 of 17 shooting from three point distance and just 27 bench points in Game 1 of their first round series.

When their vaunted offense seemingly out of synch because of the Dallas perimeter defense, the Spurs turned to the guy who'd carried the team in the last 17 seasons: Tim Duncan.

Duncan turned back the hands of time with a virtuoso performance that netted him 27 points to lead the Spurs back from a 10-point fourth quarter deficit to take the home opener 90-85 on April 20, 2014, despite the team's overall offensive struggles. Parker was second on the team in scoring with 21 points, but Ginobili (17) and Leonard (11) were the only other double-digit scorers for the Spurs. Dallas refused to lie down and allow Duncan and the Spurs to dominate them, though. Instead, they stormed to a 113-92 blowout win in Game 2 on April 23, 2014, to steal the home court advantage from San Antonio, and then hacked out a thrilling 109-108 win on April 26, 2014 including a near-improbable three-point shot from Vince Carter as time expired from about 22 feet away from the basket.

Suddenly, the mighty Spurs faced an early 1-2 deficit against a determined and inspired Dallas Mavericks squad. Once again, the Spurs turned to Duncan to save them as the Big Fundamental came up with back-to-back double-double games of 14 points and 11 rebounds during the team's 93-89 win on April 28, 2014, followed by having 16 points and 12 rebounds in a 109-103 win over the Mavericks on April 30, 2014. San Antonio regained the upper hand at 3-2. Dallas would storm back to win game six and send the series to a deciding Game 7 in San Antonio. Yet, just when the world thought that the Mavs had a clear shot at upending the Spurs, San Antonio had saved its best for last.

The Spurs made 26 of their 38 shots in the first half and virtually ran the Mavericks off the court. The final score was a brutal 119-96 on May 4, 2014. Duncan played just 30 minutes, but shot seven of eight from the field to end the series with 15 points, eight rebounds, and two blocks as the Spurs headed to the second round to face the upstart Portland Trail Blazers. The Blazers were a dangerous young team who, like the Spurs, had great three-point specialists and were led by a dynamic point guard. They had just beaten the Houston Rockets with Damian Lillard's buzzer beating three-pointer which was heard all over the world. They called that moment 'Rip City Revival,' after the

91

Blazers advanced to the second round of the NBA Playoffs for the first time in 14 years. However, Portland's renaissance was to be cut short as the Blazers ran into a brick wall named San Antonio.

The Spurs romped away with the first three games by an average winning margin of 18.66 points. Duncan rode his teammates' hot hands in the first two games. In Game 1 on May 6, 2014, it was Parker leading the team with 33 points and nine assists and Belinelli having 19 points off the bench in a 116-92 win. Duncan had only nine field goal attempts in 24 and a half minutes to score 12 points and collected 11 rebounds. During Game 2 on May 8, 2014, Duncan made four of 10 from the field to score 10 points while the team was led by Leonard's 20 points and 16 points respectively from Parker and Ginobili during a 114-97 win.

All of that came before Duncan would have an eight out of 18 shooting performance that earned him 19 points in the series-breaking Game 3 win on May 10,

2014, collecting seven rebound and four assists to help support Parker's 29 points. The Blazers would salvage a 103-92 win in Game 4 on May 12, 2014, but Duncan went for 16 points and eight rebounds in the Game 5 win, 104-82, on May 14, 2014. This would lead the Spurs back to the Western Conference Finals where they would meet their arch-nemeses the Oklahoma City Thunder who were having an MVP season from the NBA's leading scorer, Kevin Durant.

The key to the series against the Thunder was Serge Ibaka's injury. The Thunder's defensive anchor suffered a calf injury during their previous series against the Los Angeles Clippers and he was forced to sit out the first two games of the Western Conference Finals. With Ibaka out, Tim Duncan went to town by averaging 20.5 points and 9.5 rebounds to lead San Antonio to an early 2-0 series lead. Duncan started the series with 27 points after making 11 of 19 from the field (57.9 percent) in the 122-105 win on May 19, 2014. Duncan would follow that performance with yet another postseason double-double after scoring 14 points and collecting 12 rebounds securing the win for San Antonio after defeating the Thunder 112-77 on May 21, 2014.

Ibaka hobbled his way back to play in the next games and the inspired Thunder tied the series at 2-2. He had 15 points in the 106-97 win during Game 3 on May 25, 2014 and had a nine point, eight rebound game in support of Russell Westbrook scoring 40 points and Durant having 31 of his own in a 105-92 victory on May 27, 2014.

Needing a big win, the Spurs turned to Duncan again and the big man delivered 22 points and 12 rebounds after making eight of 13 from the field (61.5 percent) and six of seven free throws to put the Spurs on the verge of advancing to the Finals for the second consecutive season with a 117-89 win on May 29, 2014. Duncan poured in a mammoth 19 points and 16 rebounds in a performance where he made 42.9 percent from the field during the 112-107 series-clinching win in Game 6 on May 31, 2014. The Spurs marched to the 2014 NBA Finals against the defending champions the Miami Heat who were their conquerors in the previous season.

Game 1 of the 2014 NBA Finals turned controversial after the air-conditioning failure at the AT&T Center forced Heat superstar and reigning MVP LeBron James to play only five minutes in the fourth quarter due to cramps. James left the game with cramps at the 7:31 mark of the final period but returned to action with 3:59 left. After scoring on a driving lay-up, James left the game for good, limping to the bench. With James missing significant time, the Spurs outscored Miami 36-17 in the final period to win 110-95 on June 5, 2014, taking a 1-0 lead in their best-of-seven championship series. That incident overshadowed a spectacular performance by the ageless Tim Duncan who scored 21 points and grabbed 10 rebounds in just 33 minutes of action while being almost perfect with nine of 10 field goals and three of four free throws, helping the Spurs overcome a seven point fourth quarter lead.

Duncan would have another great outing in Game 2 on June 8, 2014, scoring 18 points and grabbing 15 rebounds while making seven of 14 from the field to shoot 50 percent. The game belonged to the Heat as they had 35 points from LeBron James and a clutch three-pointer from Chris Bosh to highlight his 18 points. With the win, LeBron not only redeemed himself from Game 1, which was later dubbed as the "Cramps Game," but his team stole home court advantage from the seemingly invincible Spurs. More importantly, the Heat looked like they were on course to win three consecutive NBA titles.

Unfortunately for Miami fans, Game 2 proved to be the Heat's swansong performance as it was San Antonio basketball the rest of the way. In Game 3 on June 10, 2014, the Spurs played the best shooting half in NBA Finals history by shooting 25 of 33 from the field including making 19 of their first 21 shots. The

Spurs went on a 10 minute 20 seconds stretch between the first two quarters where they didn't miss a single basket. By halftime the Spurs scored an incredible 71 points and took a 21-point lead to start the 3rd quarter. Duncan took a backseat with 14 points and six rebounds as he let Kawhi Leonard take over the team. Leonard scored a team-high 29 points on just 13 field goal attempts. Leonard also made life miserable for LeBron James, who scored only eight points after the first quarter and a total of 22 markers overall. This all took place during a 111-92 victory for the Spurs in Miami.

The Spurs put the Heat on the brink of defeat as they kept their feet on the gas pedal in Game 4 on June 12, 2014. San Antonio continued to play red hot from three point territory and their ball movement was working wonders for them. In the third period, the Spurs built a 21 point lead after a dunk by Tim Duncan. Duncan ran back, emotionally pumping his fists in a rare display of emotion. The Spurs' machine was humming and they were cooking another route of the Miami Heat with a 107-86 win led by Leonard's 20 points and 14 rebounds, while Duncan had just 10 points and 11 rebounds after making four of 10 from the field.

The Heat faced a brick wall in Game 5 on June 15, 2014, at the AT&T Center in San Antonio, Texas, as no team has ever come back from a 1-to-3 deficit to win the NBA title. For the Spurs, it was the opportunity to win the title at their home court and give Tim Duncan the fifth NBA championship ring which eluded him 12 months ago. It was an opportunity for redemption and the Spurs didn't let it slip away.

The 22-year old Kawhi Leonard capped off a remarkable 2014 Finals performance with 22 points and 10 rebounds as the Spurs closed out the Miami Heat with a convincing 104-87 win in front of a raucous crowd that swarmed the AT&T Center. Duncan made five of 10 from the field and four of six free throws to score 14 points in the finale while also collecting eight rebounds and blocked two shots. Leonard was named the 2014 Finals MVP after dominating both ends of the floor from Game 3 onwards. He defended LeBron James and became the Spurs' main gunner in the final three games of the series, which the Spurs swept.

With Leonard grabbing the spotlight, Tim Duncan only took 10 shots per game in the final two games of the series and averaged just 12 points and 9 rebounds in those two wins. More than the statistics, it was the iconic fifth title that mattered most to him. Duncan now matched Kobe Bryant's total, and was one away from the legendary Michael Jordan, who had six.

For the Spurs, it was a record-setting performance in the Finals. The Spurs were the first team in NBA Finals history to win three straight games by at least a 15 point margin each. Their 14.5 average winning margin for the entire series was the largest in NBA Finals history. In 12 of their 16 total playoff wins, the

Spurs won by at least 15 points and that, too, was the most ever in the NBA playoffs. Not surprisingly, the +214 plus/minus for the playoffs was also the widest margin in NBA history.

It wasn't just the Spurs who dominated and established records. Tim Duncan also added several records to his impressive resume. For one, Duncan became the first player to start on a championship team in three different decades. Duncan also bettered Kareem Abdul Jabbar's record for most minutes in the NBA playoffs of all-time with a total of 8,902 at that time. In Game 4 of the Finals, Duncan also passed Magic Johnson for double-doubles in the playoffs of all-time by notching his 158th.

The Spurs had exacted revenge on Miami, and Duncan had finally won that fifth title which evaded him in the previous season. With one ring for each finger, Duncan has the same number of rings as the other transcendental superstar of his generation, Kobe Bryant. With this secured in his pocket and with 17 hard-played season tucked under his belt, the question was whether the Big Fundamental would return for an 18th season or if he would decide to go out on top. He was getting close to the age of 39. Duncan had been mum about returning for the 2015 season during the playoffs, refusing to be baited into the topic. After the dust cleared and the Spurs came up on top, there was no question that he would be returning for at least one more season in hopes of getting another championship ring.

Tim Duncan was definitely no longer in his prime, but after averaging 15.1 points, 9.7 rebounds and 1.9 blocks per game in just 29.2 minutes per game during the 2014 season, Duncan remained one of the most effective big men in the league. With the dominance they showed in the 2014 Finals and the consistency of winning at least 50 games since the 1999-2000 season, it was hard for Duncan to walk away, especially since the Spurs were immediately installed as favorites to win again in 2015.

Opting in to the player option of his 2012 contract meant that Duncan would take in just $10.4 million for the 2015 season, an amount which paled in comparison to Kobe Bryant's $24.5M salary. Duncan's "charitable" act enabled the Spurs to return their entire 2014 title squad after the franchise was able to re-sign two key role players in versatile forward Boris Diaw (three years, $22.5 million) and break-out guard Patty Mills (three years, $12 million). Although the Spurs had their core of Parker, Ginobili, Danny Green, and 2014 Finals MVP Kawhi Leonard in contracts, Diaw and Mills played very important roles during their title run. Shortly after the return of the entire team was finalized, long-time head coach Gregg Popovich also signed a multi-year extension to remain as their bench tactician. With the whole gang intact for one more ride, the Spurs looked forward to the 2015 season, where their goal was to win their first ever back-to-back NBA titles. The Spurs opened the pre-season with a surprise defeat to the European team, Alba

Berlin, signaling the warning that the upcoming season wasn't going to be as easy as the previous one. Big man Tiago Splitter was out with a calf injury while Kawhi Leonard suffered an eye infection after their next game versus Fenerbahçe in Turkey. When the season opened, the two were on the injured list along with back-up guard Patty Mills.

As a result, the Spurs opened the season 2-3, but the injury bug refused to leave. 2014 Finals MVP Kawhi Leonard returned to action in their second game, but sharpshooter Marco Belinelli went down with a groin injury on that same night. After that shaky start, the Spurs won 10 of their next 11 games to finish the month of November. Tony Parker led that charge, averaging 17 points per game on 50 percent field goal shooting.

On November 14, 2014, Duncan scored his 25,000th career point to become the 19th player in league history to top that mark during a 93-80 win over the Los Angeles Lakers. As expected, Popovich paced

Duncan as the wins started to come. The 38-year-old played an average of 29.8 minutes per game in the month of November and averaged just 13.8 points and 9.8 rebounds per game.

The next full month saw a brutal schedule of 18 games that had the Spurs play five back-to-back pairings. Tony Parker injured his hamstring on December 5, 2014, while Leonard went out again with a hand injury on December 10, 2014. Popovich had no choice but to utilize Duncan more. He let his aging superstar play 14 of the 18 games at an average of 34.8 minutes per game to keep the injured team afloat. Duncan responded by turning in a double-double average in December at 17.9 points and 11.1 rebounds. That month would become Duncan's most prolific month of the season, but on the other hand, it would become the Spurs' first losing month in the Tim Duncan era. One of his best games of the month was on December 19, 2014 during a 129-119 loss visiting the Memphis Grizzlies. Duncan scored 32 points after making 12 out of 24 from the field and also eight of nine free throws. He also had 10 rebounds, four blocks, three assists, and two steals.

Kawhi Leonard was out for most of January while Tony Parker, Manu Ginobili, and Tim Duncan weren't as sharp as they had been the previous month. Despite their struggles, the Spurs managed to go 10-4 during the first month of 2015. Duncan played all 14 games, but his minutes were once again restricted to 26.3 per game. However, Duncan was named one of the seven reserves to the Western Conference All-Star team after averaging 14.7 points, 10.1 rebounds and 2.0 blocks per game thus far in the 2015 season, the most productive of any player with his age and length of stay in the NBA.

The selection was the 15th in Duncan's career and tied him with Shaquille O'Neal for fourth most in NBA annals. Only Kareem Abdul-Jabbar (19), Kobe Bryant (17) and Julius Erving (16) have more All-Star selections than Duncan. Aside from that, it also marked the 36th time in 39 seasons where the Spurs had sent at least one player to the mid-season classic – the most individual years among all NBA teams. On February 19, 2015, Duncan passed Denver Nuggets scoring machine Alex English at number 16 in the NBA's All-Time scoring list.

As the second half of the season started, the Spurs lost four games in a row immediately after the All-Star break, including a surprising loss to the Utah Jazz. That four-game losing streak was their second of the season and marked the first time since Duncan was drafted that they had two 4-game losing streaks in a single season. The Spurs would finish the annual Rodeo Road Trip with a losing record for the first time ever. They were 75-34 in the RRT in the previous 13 years and were a total of +423 points over their opponents during that period. This season, though, was one of injuries and struggles.

On March 4, 2014, Duncan overtook Nate Thurmond for ninth place in the NBA's All-Time rebounding list.

Two days later, Duncan blocked three shots against the Denver Nuggets and passed Patrick Ewing to become the 6th best All-Time shot blocker in NBA history. Still, the Spurs languished in the bottom half of the West's playoff picture and they needed a strong finishing kick if they were to defend their 2014 title, and they did just that. The Spurs ended the month of February with 23 losses and they finished the regular season with 27 losses. Tony Parker and Kawhi Leonard were playing their best basketball of the season while Tim Duncan continued to play sub-30 minutes per game in the final two months of the season. With the Golden State Warriors breaking away from the pack, number two was the highest they could get to and with the strong finishing kick. The chance to finish at that rank was in their hands in the final game of the regular season.

All the Spurs needed to do was win their final game of the regular season against the New Orleans Pelicans to secure the second seed. The Pelicans were playing not for positioning, but just to get to the playoffs: they needed to beat the Spurs to clinch the eighth seed over the Thunder. In a surprise, the Pelicans would down the Spurs, 108-103 to advance to the playoffs for the first time since 2011. The loss not only snapped the Spurs' 11-game winning streak, it also stopped Duncan's consecutive 20-10 games at two. Duncan would finish with 15 points and 10 boards in the losing effort. The Spurs would finish the regular season with a record of 55-27, but with the strength of the Western Conference, that was only good enough for the sixth spot in the playoffs. However, the Spurs brought along with them the momentum of 11 wins in their last 12 games to the playoffs.

It was awkward to see the Spurs play Game 1 of the first round of the playoffs on the road, but for the Clippers, it was just what they wanted. Before a sold out crowd of 19,309 at the Staples Center, Chris Paul shot 13-20 from the field en route to 32 points, seven rebounds, and six assists. The Clippers stunned the defending world champions 107-92 in Game 1 on April 19, 2015. The Spurs bounced back with a record-breaking Game 2 from Tim Duncan.

While making 14 of 23 from the field (60.9 percent) on April 22, 2015, Duncan scored 28 points and grabbed 11 rebounds in a 111-107 overtime win that tied the series at one apiece and took the home court advantage away from the Clippers. Duncan became the third player aged 38 and above to post a 28-11 stat line in the postseason. The others were Karl Malone and Kareem Abdul-Jabbar. That 20-10 performance was the 100th in his playoff career, making Duncan only the fourth player in NBA history to achieve such a feat. Duncan's 44 minutes of playing time in Game 2 was the most in the playoffs for a player aged 38 or older. Only Karl Malone's 44 minutes at age 40 in Game 1 of the 2004 Finals topped that. During that game, Duncan also became the 5th player in NBA history to score at least 5,000 total points in the playoffs.

After being held to just four points in a Game 3 defeat, Duncan posted back-to-back 20-10 nights as the teams split victories. Duncan scored 22 points and grabbed 14 rebounds in a Game 4 loss (114-105) on April 26, 2015, while he had 21 points and 11 boards in a Game 5 victory, 111-107 on April 28, 2015. Duncan shot eight out of 13 from the field in both games and his block on Blake Griffin in the final minute of Game 5 helped seal the win. The stubborn Clippers refused to fade in the sunset and stormed back to win Game 6 in San Antonio. Clippers stars Chris Paul and Blake Griffin came up big in the 2nd half to lead L.A. to a 102-96 win.

With their season on the line, Tim Duncan put up his fourth-highest scoring game of the season with 27 points on top of 11 rebounds. In a game that was played at around the same time as boxing's Floyd Mayweather, Jr. fought Manny Pacquiao in Las Vegas, the Spurs and Clippers delivered one of the best Game 7s in NBA playoff history. Both teams battled to the end and traded big shot after big shot in the final minutes. Duncan made two free throws to tie the game at 109, but that only set up Chris Paul's heroic driving bank shot that broke the tie and sent the Clippers through to the second round. It wasn't how Duncan and the Spurs wanted their season to end. Two games before, they won another crucial Game 5 and took a 3-2 lead. This time around, they blew it, and with it perhaps the final title game in the Tim Duncan era.

The Spurs 2015 free agency started with the departure of big man Tiago Splitter, whom the Spurs traded to the Atlanta Hawks to free up some $8.5 million in cap space, which they needed to have a chance to land free agent LaMarcus Aldridge. The Spurs also allowed Splitter's back-up, Australian Aron Baynes to sign with the Detroit Pistons and guard Cory Joseph to go to the Toronto Raptors. The following day, Tim Duncan confirmed that he would be returning for his 19th season and this announcement would be one of the key factors in the Spurs free agency because it would be one of the key decisions that would sway Aldridge to go to San Antonio.

On July 4, 2015, Aldridge confirmed via his Twitter account that he would be joining the San Antonio Spurs. Prior to that, the Spurs had already secured the services of Kawhi Leonard and Danny Green. Green was signed to a reported four-year $45 million deal while Leonard got a $90 million contract. However, Leonard's case was unique because he hadn't signed a formal deal yet so that his cap hold of $7.2 million would be retained. That was also a key figure in being able to offer Aldridge his maximum salary contract. A couple of days later, the Spurs signed veteran forward David West to his minimum, despite the fact that West had a $12.9 million player option to return to the Indiana Pacers. On the next day, it was also confirmed by Manu Ginobili that he would be returning for another two seasons. So in a span of six days, the Spurs re-signed Kawhi Leonard, Danny Green, Tim Duncan, and Manu Ginobili while at the same time adding LaMarcus Aldridge and David West in an unprecedented move, thus sparking the Las Vegas odds makers to install the Spurs as the number two favorite to win the 2016 NBA title. The Cavaliers are still the odds-on favorite to win the 2016 NBA title at 11/4, but the Spurs climbed from 10/1 to 9/2. Nevertheless, the recent player movements have given Tim Duncan bigger reasons to look forward to his 19th season. It also gives him the opportunity to chase a sixth NBA title, which would separate him from Kobe Bryant, who has five, and put him alongside Michael Jordan, who won six NBA championships.

Now about to turn the age of 40 years old, Duncan hasn't made any public announcements that this will be his final season. Who is to say that he wouldn't decide to leave the world of professional basketball if he was able to win the sixth NBA championship? In the first 30 games of the season, Duncan has shown his age as he been mostly kept between 20 and 30 minutes per game and hasn't scored 20 or more points at this point in the 2015-16 NBA season. However, he still has nearly 10 double-doubles in less than half of the NBA regular season because of his strong ability to collect rebounds.

On November 28, 2015, Duncan was strong inside the paint with 18 rebounds (15 on defense) while only scoring 10 points after making five of nine from the field (55.6 percent) during 108-88 win over the Atlanta Hawks. He didn't really take too many shot opportunities with Leonard continuing to be a new presence at six-foot-seven and playing as a small forward. Duncan's best offensive performance was on January 6, 2016 during a 123-98 win over the Utah Jazz where he made eight out of 13 from the field (61.5 percent) to finish with 18 points, eight rebounds, and six assists.

During their home game against the Milwaukee Bucks on December 2, 2015, the Spurs would get a 95-70 win where Duncan had an extremely efficient night of shooting with seven of 11 made from the field (63.6

percent) to finish with 16 points and 10 rebounds. The only game where he had a better field goal percentage was during the November 11, 2015 game where he would make five of seven field goals (71.4 percent) during a 113-101 win on the road against the Portland Trail Blazers, which came shortly after a 114-94 win over the Charlotte Hornets on November 7, 2015. He had just 11 points while collecting eight rebounds in a game where he would make four of five from the field and just three of four free throws.

While Leonard has been scoring more points with veterans like Duncan, Ginobili and Parker getting closer and closer to retirement, part of the Spurs' future features a six-foot-nine power forward David West who was starting to collect more of the rebounds while Duncan continued to play limited minutes in what is likely a plan by Coach Popovich to conserve one of his best players for the second part of the season, which will act as the final push for the NBA Playoffs that year.

Moving forward through the first half of 2016, there's a good chance that San Antonio is going to continue to push towards the first seed in the Western Conference, even though the Golden State Warriors won 33 out of their first 35 games of the current NBA season. The Warriors are also the defending NBA Champions from the 2014-15 season and went on an impressive 24-game winning streak to start the season.

Chapter 7: International Experience

In the early stages of Duncan's basketball career, he was one of the members of the United States men's basketball team during the 1994 Goodwill Games held in St. Petersburg, Russia, which were created in an effort to improve the relationship between the U.S. and Soviet Union while also inviting many other countries to the event. Duncan and the U.S. team would win the bronze medal in the tournament. He would also find some experience during two separate International Basketball Federation (FIBA) Americas Championships.

The United States would win a gold medal in both of the 1999 FIBA Tournaments of the Americas – months after Duncan helped the Spurs win an NBA championship in just his second season as a professional in the NBA – as they were undefeated throughout the group play round that featured a 118-72 win over Uruguay on July 15, 1999, and a 94-60 win over Canada on July 16, 1999. The U.S. continued their winning streak in the quarterfinal pool round with another four wins that featured a 90-73 win over Brazil on July 20, 1999, and a 116-76 victory over Puerto Rico on July 22, 1999. This was followed up with an 88-59 win during the semifinals on July 23, 1999, and a 92-66 win over Canada for the United States to earn their fourth reign as the Tournament of the Americas champions.

Duncan would make a return to Team Red, White and Blue for the 2003 Tournament of Americas inside the Roberto Clemente Coliseum in San Juan, Puerto Rico. The United States would once again go undefeated in play against the rest of Group B, starting with Duncan having 17 points and six rebounds during a 110-76 win over Brazil on August 20, 2003. Duncan wouldn't have to be much of a factor in the second game of group play on August 21, 2003, with just six points during a 111-73 win against the Dominican Republic. He would bounce back with 13 points after making five out of 10 from the field and also had 13 rebounds and five assists during a 98-68 win over Venezuela on August 22, 2003. He would sit out during the August 23, 2003, game against the U.S. Virgin Islands (113-55). The U.S. team was moving onto the quarterfinal group of the tournament.

On August 25, 2003, Duncan was able to score 16 points after making five of nine field goals and all six shots from the foul line to help the United States defeat their neighbors to the North in Canada, 111-71. Duncan would find himself in a game against teammate Manu Ginobili and Argentina on August 26, 2003, but he would make seven of 12 field goals (58.3 percent) and five of six free throws to score 19 points to go with nine rebounds, six assists, three steals, and two blocked shots in a 94-86 win. Duncan would have another 16 points and six rebounds during a 96-69 win over Mexico on August 27, 2003, and then another 16 points and nine rebounds during a 91-65 victory against Puerto Rico on August 28, 2003.

After a few days of rest, the United States would play Puerto Rico again on August 30, 2003, in a game where Duncan made five of 11 field goals (45.5 percent) to finish with 14 points, eight rebounds, and three assists during an 87-71 win over Puerto Rico to advance to the gold medal game. In the finals on August 31, 2003, Duncan led the United States with 23 points after making 11 out of 15 from the field (73.3 percent) while also collecting 14 rebounds and three assists in the 106-73 win.

It was an impressive end to the FIBA Tournament of the Americas for Duncan, who would later become one of the members of the final roster that would represent the United States during the 2004 Summer Olympic Games held in Athens, Greece. Duncan was, at this point, one of the veteran players on a roster that also featured LeBron James, Carmelo Anthony and Dwayne Wade.

Unfortunately, the United States would not have the same success that they found in the Americas competition, losing the first match in Group B play on August 15, 2004, against Puerto Rico, 92-73. Duncan had a double-double in the loss with 15 points and 16 rebounds while also collecting five steals and four assists in the contest. The United States would bounce back on August 17, 2004 with a 77-71 victory over home team Greece. Duncan led the game with nine rebounds while also scoring 14 points while Allen Iverson scored 17 points to lead the team. Duncan would led the United States with 18 points and 11 rebounds on August 19, 2004, during an 89-79 win over Australia. Iverson and Shawn Marion each scored 16 points in the game as well.

Duncan would score 16 points and 12 rebounds on August 21, 2004, but Lithuania would get the 94-90 win thanks to Šarūnas Jasikevičius leading everyone with 28 points in the group play match. The United States was able to rebound with an 89-53 rout of Angola on August 23, 2004, led by Duncan scoring 15 points and collecting seven rebounds and just two assists. The United States would finish with a 3-2 record in Group B and that was just enough to earn a berth into the knockout round.

During the quarterfinals on August 26, 2004, the United States defeated Spain 102-94 despite Spain's Pau Gasol scoring 29 points in the contest. Stephon Marbury would lead everyone with 31 points, followed by Iverson (16 points), Carlos Boozer (12 points) and Lamar Odom (11 points). Duncan himself scored just nine points while collecting four rebounds and two assists. The U.S. would struggle in the semifinal round on August 27, 2003 with an 89-81 loss to Argentina. Marbury led the team with 18 points while Duncan had 10 points and six rebounds; Duncan's San Antonio teammate Ginobili led Argentina with 29 points. The United States would be able to exact some revenge against Lithuania with a 104-96 win in the bronze medal game where Duncan was limited to scoring six points and had eight rebounds. Marion led the team with 22 points, followed by Iverson's 15 points and 14 points from both Marbury and Odom.

Chapter 8: Duncan's Personal Life

In a league of talkers, braggers, and swaggerers, Duncan is famous for his quiet, stoic personality. He is sponsored by Adidas, but he is not an icon in the shoe or fashion world unlike other NBA stars such as Michael Jordan or Allen Iverson. Probably the most well-known Tim Duncan commercials are not for Adidas or some other global brand, but rather H-E-B, a Texas grocery chain. We know surprisingly little about Tim Duncan off the basketball court, and he probably likes it that way.

Duncan may not show up at celebrity glam fests or major commercials, but he does possess a life off the basketball court. During the offseason, Duncan normally returns to his home in the Virgin Islands. He swims, runs, bikes, and spends time with friends and family in the warm Caribbean sun. He does everything but play basketball. There are advantages to this from a basketball perspective. In addition to mentally unwinding from the grind of an NBA season, playing other sports builds up other muscles which are not used as much in basketball, thus ensuring a body which is as sound as his basketball fundamentals. When training camp opens, Duncan is always in shape and ready to go, invigorated by the months of rest and good exercise.

That does not mean Duncan has always ignored basketball in the offseason. Outside the NBA, Duncan has also played for Team USA, though his impact there has been much more limited. Duncan wanted to play for the Virgin Islands in the Olympics, but in 1996, he played for Team USA in the 22-and-under World Championships. International basketball rules forbid players from switching countries after playing at a senior level, so Duncan was stuck with the United States. After he missed the 2000 Olympics due to knee surgery, Duncan finally competed in the 2004 Olympics for the United States. However, that event was a disaster. Many elite American NBA players such as Kevin Garnett and Tracy McGrady sat out, citing concerns about terrorism during the first Summer Olympics since the September 11 attacks. Duncan struggled with the different officiating between FIBA and NBA ball, and the roster was poorly staffed with elite athletes, but poor shooters. Team USA would be humiliated and receive the bronze medal in the 2004 Olympics. While this was a painful memory for Duncan, the defeat spurred Team USA to pay more attention to international ball and not just blithely assume that they would win every year. In 2008, the USA would send the "Redeem Team" which would grab the gold medal back.

Outside of sports altogether, Duncan is known for his nerdy tendencies. A video game player who likes to play as himself in basketball games, he also has a tattoo of Merlin on his chest, plays Dungeons and Dragons and has dressed up for Renaissance Faires in the past. Tim is also the frequent target of The Onion, a fake news website which pokes fun at his unassuming, intelligent personality with headlines such as "Tim Duncan Calls Out Geometric Angle Needed to Make Bank Shot" or "Tim Duncan Hams it Up For Crowd by Arching Left Eyebrow Slightly."

Chapter 9: Impact on Basketball

As Tim Duncan enters the final years of his career, some may wonder whether he has left any real impact on the basketball court. His trademark move, the bank jumper off the glass, is so simple that middle school basketball players learn it. Duncan never had a single moment which lives on into legend like Wilt Chamberlain's 100-point game, Magic Johnson's skyhook against the Celtics, Michael Jordan's Last Shot in the 1998 NBA Finals, or more recently LeBron James's demolition of the Boston Celtics in Game 6 of the 2012 NBA Playoffs. Tim Duncan, as so many complained over the years, is often characterized as a boring player leading a boring team.

While Tim Duncan may not be remembered for flashy highlights or games where he utterly destroyed his opponents, he has left the simplest, yet most important impact of all: he won basketball games. Duncan was always willing to do whatever it took to win, no matter the circumstances or reward. When he was called upon to serve as the defensive anchor for a slow, tough San Antonio team, he delivered. When he was called upon to be one of the focal points to a faster Spurs team, which emphasized offensive spacing, he delivered. When he was called upon as a rookie to be the franchise player of a Spurs aiming for a title the minute he was drafted, and when he was called upon over a decade later to be just a piece in the San Antonio team, he delivered. Duncan has always done whatever he has been called upon to do, whenever required. He never complained about a lack of minutes, the burden of carrying a franchise, the lack of quality teammates before Parker and Ginobili became All-Stars, or about anything else.

By working hard, sacrificing for the good of the team, and never complaining, Duncan set an example for the rest of the Spurs to follow. Manu Ginobili, for years Duncan's best teammate, was placed on the bench early in his career. Gregg Popovich's goal was to limit

Ginobili's minutes as well as ensure a strong bench. Many shooting guards worse than Ginobili would have chafed at playing such a role, but Ginobili has accepted not being part of the starting lineup for several years at this point. Tony Parker was a 19-year old Frenchmen when he arrived with the San Antonio Spurs. Popovich was frustrated with the young Parker's inconsistency and poor decision-making, and hounded him again and again in practice to improve. Parker sometimes grew frustrated over this constant scolding, but he never gave up or folded under the pressure. He knew that while Popovich was tough on him, he was even harder on Duncan in practice, even though Duncan, at that point, had already won a Finals MVP award and made the All-NBA First Team multiple times.

Duncan never complained, and Parker and Ginobili knew that if the great Tim Duncan never complained, they had no right to either. So rather than fight against Popovich, they listened to their coach's instructions.

Today, Tony Parker has made 6 All-Star Teams, has made the All-NBA team three times, and is one of the best point guards in the NBA. Manu Ginobili has made the All-Star team twice and will almost certainly make the Basketball Hall of Fame. Both of them, despite their own talents and hard work, would be the first to declare that Duncan set an example that made them the great players that they continue to be today.

It is not just stars like Ginobili and Parker who have benefited from the example that Duncan has set. Year in and year out, the Spurs have molded players such as Danny Green, Stephen Jackson, and Derek Anderson into valuable role players. All of these players who came through San Antonio have cited Duncan's hard work and leadership as an important influence in the development of their careers. Duncan has never cared about his individual numbers over the years, and he has imparted that attitude to the Spurs organization as a whole. Duncan may not have done anything that no one has ever seen or will ever see again, but his impact is not through making something new. He has refined the time-honored lessons of hard work, putting the team ahead of the individual, and leadership – and that is an impact far more valuable than any new move or lesson.

Chapter 10: Tim Duncan's Legacy and Future

In 2009, Duncan sat down for an interview with Bill Russell. Arguably the greatest player in NBA history aside from Jordan, Russell won 11 championship rings with the Boston Celtics in the 1950s and 1960s, a turbulent era for a rising black basketball player. The two of them talked of the similarities of their games, of the importance of psychology on the basketball court, of how they got along with their coach, and of the importance of winning awards even though the two shared 7 MVPs between them. Russell called Duncan his "favorite athlete" and noted how Duncan was capable of playing with almost anyone. That interview sums up Duncan's legacy better than any words can proclaim – he was someone who could always work within the team, always did what it took to win, and had no weaknesses whatsoever.

All good things come to an end, and eventually so will Tim Duncan's days in the NBA. He is now 38 years old. Very few Hall of Fame big men have continued to be so successful at such an age. Hakeem Olajuwon and Shaquille O'Neal were barely hanging on in the league at that age, and Bill Russell had retired at 35. So when will Duncan's days be up? Will it be when he wins a fifth championship? Will it be when his current contract expires in 2015? Or perhaps it will be at the end of this NBA season? His former great teammate David Robinson announced his retirement at the beginning of the 2002-03 season, transforming it into a farewell tour that inspired the Spurs to their 2nd championship. Will Duncan do the same? Or will he just quietly announce it at a press conference at the end of this season, or next season, or sometime in the future, before riding off into the sunset like the cowboys of old?

It is impossible to tell, for Duncan has remained as ageless as ever. He barely looks older than he did as a rookie with the San Antonio Spurs. In fact, with his decision to regrow his hair in the 2014 season onwards, you could even argue that he looks younger! While he may play fewer minutes than ever before, especially with LaMarcus Aldridge on board for the 2015-16 season, Duncan's production per minute has barely dropped, even compared to his MVP prime. This is despite the fact that he has averaged less than 30 minutes of playing time in four of the last five regular seasons. As the 2015-2016 season is about to start, Duncan is coming off a season where he was named 3rd Team All-NBA, 17 years after he was named to his first All-NBA 1st team. Not only that, Duncan also made it to the NBA's All-Defensive 2nd team for the 7th time in his career last season.

With his longevity, statistics, leadership, championships, and awards, Tim Duncan is undisputedly the greatest power forward of all time. He may no longer be able to carry the Spurs singlehandedly to a title like he did in 2003, but he is still one of the best players on the most disciplined team in the league, a discipline which exists thanks to Duncan himself. Regardless of the cheers and roars of the crowd, regardless of teammates, regardless of the pressure and difficulty of changing from a defensive-styled team to an offensive team, Tim Duncan has come through again and again. As he prepares to enter his twilight years, it is that above all else which he can remain proud of.

Final Word/About the Author

I was born and raised in Norwalk, Connecticut. Growing up, I could often be found spending many nights watching basketball, soccer, and football matches with my father in the family living room. I love sports and everything that sports can embody. I believe that sports are one of most genuine forms of competition, heart, and determination. I write my works to learn more about influential athletes in the hopes that from my writing, you the reader can walk away inspired to put in an equal if not greater amount of hard work and perseverance to pursue your goals. If you enjoyed *Tim Duncan: The Inspiring Story of Basketball's Greatest Power Forward*, please leave a review! Also, you can read more of my works on *LaMarcus Aldridge, Derrick Rose, Paul George, Kevin Garnett, Michael Jordan, LeBron James, Kyrie Irving, Klay Thompson, Stephen Curry, Kevin Durant, Russell Westbrook, Chris Paul, Blake Griffin, Kobe Bryant,*

Anthony Davis, Joakim Noah, Scottie Pippen, Carmelo Anthony, Kevin Love, Grant Hill, Tracy McGrady, Vince Carter, Patrick Ewing, Karl Malone, Tony Parker, Allen Iverson, Hakeem Olajuwon, Reggie Miller, Michael Carter-Williams, James Harden, John Wall, Tim Duncan, Steve Nash, J.J. Watt, Colin Kaepernick, Aaron Rodgers, Tom Brady, Russell Wilson, and *Peyton Manning* in the Kindle Store. If you love basketball, check out my website at claytongeoffreys.com to join my exclusive list where I let you know about my latest books and give you lots of goodies.

Like what you read?

I write because I love sharing the stories of influential athletes like Tim Duncan with fantastic readers like you. My readers inspire me to write more so please do not hesitate to let me know what you thought by leaving a review! If you love books on life, basketball, or productivity, check out my website at claytongeoffreys.com to join my exclusive list where I let you know about my latest books. Aside from being the first to hear about my latest releases, you can also download a free copy of *33 Life Lessons: Success Principles, Career Advice & Habits of Successful People.* See you there!

Made in the USA
San Bernardino, CA
04 April 2016